Phantasy in Childhood

First published in 1952, *Phantasy in Childhood* is for a psycho-analytically oriented public. The authors have set out to express in non-technical language some of the theories we owe to the work of Melanie Klein, and to show how they are repeatedly borne out in the day-to-day behaviour of children. Numerous practical examples are given, drawn from experience of children under many different conditions. In some cases the authors merely suggest interpretations which seem likely, but would need psychoanalytic confirmation; in others the meaning is unmistakable from the material available; in all, the aim has been to point to the presence and nature of unconscious phantasy, and to its expression in behaviour. Although written in simple language, the book is not easy, as, to those who are unfamiliar with it, the concept of unconscious phantasy is in itself difficult. The attempt has been made, however, to give living pictures of the children, and, while definitely not advocating the wild application of a psycho-analytic technique, to show how some understanding of the importance of phantasy can be of value to those caring for children.

This book is a re-issue originally published in 1952. The language used is a reflection of its era and no offence is meant by the Publishers to any reader by this re-publication.

Phantasy in Childhood

Audrey Davidson and Judith Fay

Routledge
Taylor & Francis Group
LONDON AND NEW YORK

First published in 1952
by Routledge & Kegan Paul

This edition first published in 2025 by Routledge
4 Park Square, Milton Park, Abingdon, Oxon, OX14 4RN

and by Routledge
605 Third Avenue, New York, NY 10017

Routledge is an imprint of the Taylor & Francis Group, an informa business

© 1952 Audrey Davidson and Judith Fay

Publisher's Note
The publisher has gone to great lengths to ensure the quality of this reprint but points out that some imperfections in the original copies may be apparent.

Disclaimer
The publisher has made every effort to trace copyright holders and welcomes correspondence from those they have been unable to contact.

A Library of Congress record exists under LCCN: 52004507

ISBN: 978-1-032-93750-2 (hbk)
ISBN: 978-1-003-56746-2 (ebk)
ISBN: 978-1-032-93752-6 (pbk)

Book DOI 10.4324/9781003567462

PHANTASY
IN CHILDHOOD

by

AUDREY DAVIDSON

and

JUDITH FAY

ROUTLEDGE & KEGAN PAUL
Broadway House, 68-74 Carter Lane
London

First published in 1952
by Routledge & Kegan Paul Limited
Broadway House, 68-74 Carter Lane
London E.C.4
Made and printed in Great Britain
by William Clowes and Sons Limited
London and Beccles

Contents

v

Introduction

THE material of this book has been gained over a period of fifteen years, in work with children under varied circumstances. In the case of one of us (A.D.), experience has included the running of clubs for children and adolescents in a dockland settlement, work as a psychiatric social worker in a Child Guidance Clinic, and contact with children in hospital in the course of medical training. The other of us (J.F.) is a Froebel and nursery school teacher, who has taught children of all ages in different types of schools, and has been Superintendent of a nursery school. She has acted as nurse to babies under a year in a residential nursery, has had the care of homeless children, and has been tutor to student teachers and nursery nurses. She has also worked with individual neurotic and psychotic children. The history of Dinah, given in Chapter VII, has been recorded by her mother, Elisabeth Bennett (Mrs. O'Kelly), and we should like to thank her for allowing us to make use of her very full notes.

We have set out to express in non-technical language some of the theories we owe to the work of Melanie Klein, and to show both how they are repeatedly borne out in the day-to-day behaviour of children, and how helpful some knowledge of infantile phantasies can be from a practical point of view. In an early paper, 'The Development of a Child', Mrs. Klein shows how, by observing a four-year-old boy and listening to his repeated questions, she came to recognize that his slow mental development and inhibited play were due to anxieties about sexuality. As the result of conversations in which he became more and more able to express his sexual interests and curiosity, and was given the information he sought, his anxiety diminished, and he was able to make fuller use of his intellectual powers, and to play with much greater freedom. In his play there was a release of phantasies which further confirmed her suppositions as to the source of his anxieties, and led her to a deeper understanding of his problems. As time went on, she began to point out to him some of the meanings underlying his questions, stories, and play, and it was from here that she developed her Play Technique by means of which she showed that the principles of psycho-analysis, as originated by Freud, could be applied to young children. Through it she confirmed many of Freud's discoveries concerning the unconscious mind of the young child; she also showed that much of the phantasy he had pointed to dates from early infancy, both developing and adding to his original concepts, so that much greater understanding of children is now possible. Such insight as we have gained into children's phantasies is due to the writings of Mrs. Klein and her co-workers (in particular the late Dr. Susan Isaacs) and to our own personal experiences of psychoanalysis; our application of Mrs. Klein's theories and our presentation of them in this book is, however, our own responsibility.

AUDREY DAVIDSON
JUDITH FAY

CHAPTER ONE

The World in Black and White

WHEN the glass splinter of hate enters the heart of little Kay in *The Snow Queen*, he suddenly sees everything around him which had been so pleasant as spoilt and bad. The roses look worm-eaten and disgust him; his friend Gerda's face looks ugly, and her crying annoys him. As a contrast to Kay's cruel, hard, frozen state of anger, Gerda represents warmth and love and goodness, and it is her tears that eventually melt the splinter and restore Kay to his former state of good feeling, enabling them to return to their old life of perfect friendship and happiness at home. Many fairy tales with their extremes of good and bad—of wealth and poverty, luck and misfortune, helpful friends and persecuting enemies—express universal phantasies that have their roots in infancy. Young children do tend to see things in such black-and-white terms, according to their feelings of the moment. At times the world is ideally good; at other times intensely bad.

Very early in life there is probably the experience of absolute goodness and well-being, unspoilt by memories of yesterday or anticipation of tomorrow. To the baby who has just been fed and feels warm and sleepy and satisfied, mother and along with her the whole world must appear as all-loving, all-giving, and unfailing. To try to describe a baby's feelings in ordinary verbal terms may seem absurd; even the feelings of adults cannot always be expressed satisfactorily this way, for we do not feel in words; how still more remote and inexpressible must be the feelings of infants. Yet some access to the mind of a baby, some evidence of his feelings, has been gained in recent years through the careful work that has been done in observing the exact behaviour and reactions of babies themselves, through the skilled understanding of the play of children, and through the interpretation of phantasy material produced by people of all ages in the course of psycho-analytic treatment.[1] It seems therefore worth risking inadequate verbal descriptions of feelings in order to try to understand infantile phantasies—which embody the most primitive hopes and fears, loves and hates—since they remain unconscious in the mind of the older child and the adult, and underlie not only fairy tales, daydreams and other products of the imagination, but also everyday thought and behaviour.

It is understandable that, to the baby, his mother is 'good' when he himself feels 'good'. At first, when he is not able to en-visage her as a whole person, he must be aware of her simply as a breast, good because it makes him feel contented and loved, and the warm stream of milk passing into him seems the essence of life and goodness; because in reflecting his own feelings it seems to be part of him, and because his loving feelings for it seem to *create* it as a good breast. At all ages we see examples of idealization, in which there is a conception of something wholly perfect, with blindness to any possibility of negative qualities. For instance Tony, a seven-year-old evacuee, remarked to his billet-mother in a burst of excited anticipation when going to the circus: 'My lovely sweetheart, you're the most beautiful girl in the world!' He added: 'I love you even when you're angry with me.' Nothing was further from the truth; when things went wrong with Tony, he invariably saw the adults in his world as mean and hateful, and his beautiful fairy godmother soon changed into somebody more like a dangerous old witch.

Just as the baby sees the breast (mother) as 'good' because of his

[1] See particularly the works of Melanie Klein and Susan Isaacs.

own feelings of love and contentment, so he sees her as 'bad' when he feels frustrated and angry. Almost every mother can distinguish her baby's different cries, and is soon able to recognize moments when his needs are intense, as when he is very angry, frightened, or in pain. At such a time a baby may quickly work himself up into a state of misery, rage, and panic, with the feeling that he has been utterly deserted and, in our language, as if he had been left to starve to death. For him, a temporary state of time does not exist: 'now' is 'forever'. He cannot possibly know the good reasons his mother may have for not coming to him, nor that she is doing all in her power to make him feel better, but cannot stop his feeling pain nor discover the cause of his distress. To the baby, the mother who does not come when he needs her or does not make him feel better is bad: she is not there, either in fact or as a good helpful person, while as an extension of himself she is at that moment miserable, deserted, angry and hating, attacking and attacked. As is evident from the behaviour of older children, such acts as screaming, urinating, defaecating, sucking, and swallowing, when performed in anger, can be felt to be ways of hurting people; moreover, at the very moment when in phantasy he is attacking the breast, the baby himself is often experiencing painful and unpleasant sensations: his screams may hurt his throat, his sobs may shake him violently and leave him gasping for breath, his evacuations may burn and chafe him, and his whole body may become hot and uncomfortable. One can well imagine that these discomforts may be felt by him to be attacks made on him by the breast, in retaliation for what he is doing to it, and thus it comes to be feared as retributive and dangerous. When at such a moment he is picked up, he may be too frenzied to relax or suck peacefully, and too frightened to make contact at all at first. Many babies, after a bout of angry screaming for food, refuse to take it, and one can imagine that, if the child's head is held and the nipple pushed into his mouth in spite of his resistance, his

3

phantasies of being attacked could be intensified. When, at the age of ten weeks, Dinah (who is described in Chapter VII) had been very hungry and crying angrily, she would be in a state of tension and unable to feed at first; instead she would turn from the breast and suck her own hands, or would turn her head round and round so that the nipple revolved in her mouth, clenching her hands, drumming her feet, and taking very shallow breaths, until at last she took a great gulp and began to suck. In mouthing the nipple she was perhaps testing the breast that had become bad for her, while in sucking her own hands she was turning to a substitute, less satisfying but under her control, and therefore less dangerous than the breast which, in phantasy, she had attacked in anger.

As the child grows older and his world widens, fear of punishment for his attacks on the mother is transferred to other people and objects. For instance, the common fear of being drawn down the waste-pipe of the bath or lavatory can arise from the child's phantasy of being sucked in by his mother in revenge for having greedily sucked her into him. Dinah, when showing considerable hostility towards her mother at about two years, had many phantasies of being attacked back, accusing her of biting and smacking her and of cutting her finger, while hairwashing, too, was seen as an act of cruelty by a 'horrid Mummy'. At this time she developed certain marked fears: she was afraid of not being able to get out of the bath before the plug was pulled out, and had always to pull it out herself later; she screamed in terror at the sight of a new charwoman, and was frightened when the salvage woman came to collect newspapers, repeating during the day: 'Little lady take away Mummy's papers' and later that she 'wanted to take away Dinah'. It seems possible that Dinah's fear of being taken away by the salvage woman (and perhaps, too, by the waste-pipe when her mother pulled out the plug) arose because she felt herself to be the 'little lady' who took away Mummy's papers, since (as will be discussed later in more detail) her hostility to her mother was accompanied by a preference for and close attachment to her father, whose newspaper she proudly carried up each morning. Thus the situation seemed to be one of rivalry, in which Dinah felt that she was taking away her mother's place and rights, thereby incurring her jealousy and desire to punish.

At all ages everyday situations that justifiably provoke some degree of anxiety may be embroidered and distorted by phantasy, possible real dangers being seen in terms of retribution for aggression. A clear example of this was seen one day in the case of Billy ($3\frac{1}{2}$), whose mother had doted on him until, when he was two years old, she fell in love with a man who was not her husband, lost all interest in the child, and finally deserted him, with the result that he had to be boarded out. In his relationship with his foster-mother, Billy was demanding and domineering, showing anxiety and anger if he was not able to control her just as he wished. One night in bed he clung to her, and when she was about to turn out his light shouted angrily that she was to stay till it was morning. He called her back as soon as she had left the room, saying that he was crying, and when she remarked that his eyes looked dry, replied indignantly: 'Only one eye is dry! I shall cry till blood comes!' When asked what would make blood come, he said: 'Nails and glass. My bad foot was bleeding; it hurts. *You* made it worse!' His foster-mother suggested that he felt she did nasty things to him to make him cry, such as leaving him alone at night, at which he started hitting her on the chest shouting: 'Bully! Bully!' He then immediately glanced in a frightened way at a screen in the corner of the room and whispered miserably: 'The bulls are behind there! They're coming to bite me!' Then, in a brighter tone: 'You ought to come and see the horses in the field with me!' His foster-mother got up to go again, but Billy still clung to her, calling to her to stay, and when she went to the door began to cry loudly, so that she had to come back. She said he was making such a noise that he sounded like a bull himself, but he protested: 'I'm making a noise to frighten the bull away. The bulls are over there behind the curtain.' The foster-mother then said: 'Don't you think you're the bull and this is the curtain?' pointing to one behind Billy's bed. He said in a state of excitement: 'No—they're coming down the chimney—bulls, bulldogs, bogies, horses, cats! Did you see that ginger cat? You go and see it—it's dead. Harry stroked it and it squeaked, but it's dead now.' He repeated: 'The bulls are coming to bite me!' then added in a more playful tone and with less anxiety: 'I'm Johnny biting *you*!' (Johnny being the two-year-old boy who lived next door and was going through a stage of much biting). Billy then asked in a much more cheerful voice that Joan, the older girl who shared his room, should come to bed as she would keep the bulls away, and was finally reassured when she did come, a minute or two later, and by the fact that his foster-mother removed the screen.

It was not easy for the foster-mother to see what in particular was prompting Billy's extreme anxiety at being left for the night. Clearly there was a constant interplay between his impulses to attack and his fear of being attacked: he hit his foster-mother, calling her 'bully', and was at the same time afraid of 'bulls' behind the screen, while his fear of being bitten by a bull was linked with his wish to bite her, and the threat to cry 'till blood comes' was immediately followed by the accusation that she had made his bleeding foot worse. In short, Billy felt that he was being 'bitten back', and his anxiety began to be relieved only when he was able to admit, and to express directly but in a modified form his wish to bite his foster-mother, and found that he could be accepted by her as a biting bull without harming her or turning her into one.

Later that night when Billy was asleep, the foster-mother discovered the reality situation which had aroused such anxiety in

THE WORLD IN BLACK AND WHITE

him and set fire to phantasies that were evidently so terrifying. That morning he had been for a walk with Johnny's mother, who had been much more concerned with her own baby than with Billy. During the walk he was told by an older child that some cows were bulls, and later the adult showed fear of some approaching horses and hurried the children away. Billy's new shoes were uncomfortable and made a blister on his heel which bled, and on the way home they saw a dead ginger cat in the road. It seems as if his great anxiety at being left by his foster-mother at night was linked with the anxiety he had felt in the morning when left on his own, without adult love and support, to face the frightening walk. Moreover, in identifying himself with Johnny he gained relief from becoming the child who had not been neglected and threatened with danger, which perhaps in Billy's mind was because Johnny, as the baby, could bite without incurring punishment. The salient feature of the bedtime situation, however, was that the terrors of the walk were all dramatized in terms of punishment for his attacks on his foster-mother, the outside dangers representing his own aggressive impulses from which he needed protection.

George, too, showed how dangerous the world can seem in the light of infantile phantasies of attack and punishment. His mother was a private nurse who had been deserted by her husband before George was born and had subsequently divorced him, never mentioning him again. She was always measuring George against her mental picture of an ideal son, well-mannered, charming, and self-controlled. She was afraid of his strong feelings and did her best to prevent any display of aggression on his part, generally giving in to him in a grudging way to avoid a scene. On the other hand she would vent her own anger on him if he displeased or disappointed her, and would sometimes bait him and stage a quarrel with him when she was really annoyed with someone else or frustrated over some other situation. In addition, George's behaviour and activities were necessarily limited by the fact that he had to spend a great deal of his time in the houses of people whom his mother was nursing. The result was that he had no means of testing his angry feelings and destructive wishes in everyday situations and in his play, and of discovering that they were not so dangerous as he feared. His phantasies of the power of his own aggression must have been intensified by his mother's evident fear of it, and in addition he had to cope with frightening and bewildering experiences of her anger.

When George was four years old, his mother was no longer able to get enough daily work, and so he had to go and live with his grandmother, while she worked in a hospital. Here he quickly became more aggressive and truculent in his behaviour, and very much concerned with daggers, guns, and bombs, which his mother deplored, denying the impulses that lay behind by saying that he had learnt such things from the children he played with in the street. For a time he went round the house armed with a variety of weapons, threatening with gestures to stab people to death, and he liked to discuss at great length possible ways of inflicting injury, and of torturing or killing people and animals. When made to sit quietly he often spent the time sharpening a piece of wood until he had reduced it to a heap of splinters, tearing or cutting paper into shreds, or taking a toy to bits. Sometimes when challenged or frustrated he would assault someone violently and do real injury, but most of the time he appeared guarded and defensive, as if guilty and uncertain of himself, and usually wore an unhappy, sullen, and defiant expression. What George showed so clearly was that his aggressiveness was matched by fears of attack: he expected others to behave to him exactly as he behaved or wished to behave to them. He frequently imagined he was being assaulted, and would take an innocent remark or an enquiring look to be an insult; he could be deeply injured by criticism, and hated above all to be accused of meanness and greed, particularly in regard to food, which became persecutory and un-eatable if he selfishly grabbed. One day, for instance, he had just served himself generously with a second helping of runner beans when another child who had come to lunch began taunting him about being greedy and robbing others of their share. George's face grew black, and his enjoyment of the beans was spoilt; he became progressively more disgusted by them, and finally said he could not eat them because they were green snakes and beginning to crawl. As we shall see later, food which had be-come persecutory to George was often seen by him as something alive. He was also much concerned with the question of defence against wild animals, and frequently talked about what might happen if they escaped from their cages. There was no doubt that he felt himself to be surrounded by dangerous enemies, and that some of his apparently unprovoked aggression was a defence against attack.

After George had been with his grandmother for a few months he started boasting about his Uncle Bill, who, although based to some extent on a real uncle with whom George had had some contact as a baby, was clearly for the most part imaginary. Like George himself, Uncle Bill was constantly being fiercely attacked, but on account of his immense strength and magic qualities was always able to overcome his enemies, and performed many wonderful exploits; for instance, the huge whale which George saw at the Natural History Museum was, he said, the one Uncle Bill killed with a penknife. Uncle Bill protected George from danger and was used as a threat against his enemies; he upheld all George's activities and always exonerated him from blame ('Uncle Bill doesn't mind boys hitting boys with hammers'). At the same time he was extremely stern with other children and a firm upholder of fair play: for example, when the boy next door was being reprimanded for hitting a smaller child, George said: 'My Uncle Bill has boys my own size for me to fight.' Uncle Bill also possessed an abundance of material things, with the result that George did not have to feel persecuted by objects he saw in shop windows and could not have; instead he would proudly boast: 'My Uncle Bill has all the bicycles in the world.' Clearly, Uncle Bill was a strong controlling force who acted as a safeguard against George's own aggressive impulses—the wild animals who might escape from their cages. He was George's attempt to deal with his guilt over his aggressiveness, providing him with boys the right size to be fought and permitting him to hit with hammers; at the same time he protected George from destruction by those he had attacked (little boys must not be hit by big boys). Also, as an idealized father-figure, he was a reassurance to George that his early destructive wishes against his father had not, after all, been strong enough to kill him or send him away, or turn him into a retaliating persecutor. The fact that George had no real father to allay his dread about the power of angry feelings, while his mother evidently feared them, must have intensified his problems, as it was certainly his own aggressive impulses and phantasies which lay at the root of his feelings of persecution.

This confusion, so common in childhood, between what really happens, what is actually done, and what is simply wished or feared, emanates from early infantile phantasies. Angry feelings do seem to have the power to hurt, to do real physical injury, and loving feelings to comfort and do good, such concepts being embodied in the fairy story of *The Sleeping Beauty*, in which the wishes of the good fairies make the princess grow up beautiful and accomplished, while the curse of the bad fairy brings her to a state close to death. In the interplay of conflicting feelings, the external world—the child's environment of home and school, parents and teachers—serves partly as a stage on which he dramatizes his phantasies, and partly as a touchstone by means of which he is gradually able to find out where the real thing differs from what he feels it to be. In George's case the omnipotent phantasy-figure, Uncle Bill, unmodified by contact with a real father, gradually faded in importance when later George made a relationship with Mr. B., a mild father-substitute who did much to help him make links with reality. Again and again the ideally perfect person is matched against the harsh, revengeful one, the fairy queen against the witch, the prince against the ogre, and the child has to keep testing the real parents to find out how far they correspond with his phantasies. The fact that it is disturbing for him to have the two extremes contained in one person was illustrated by Harry (4), who had been deserted by his mother and was boarded out. He remarked one night to his foster-mother, on whom he greatly depended: 'I hope the fairy doesn't come.' Harry's fairies were bad: they scratched or 'schlonked' him, and were sometimes said to be red or blue, which seemed to make them more frightening. The foster-mother suggested that perhaps she was the bad fairy, as she seemed bad to Harry on the frequent occasions when he was angry with her and abused her, and that he might feel that when the good person went away at night the bad one came in. Harry looked at her earnestly and anxiously and said: 'Yes, it's you', and then was silent. Suddenly he burst out laughing, exclaiming with relief: 'You're only pretending!' It seemed as if he could not bear for more than a moment to recognize that the bad fairy and the good foster-mother were the same person, and had quickly to deny it. Sometimes a child will make a nurse, teacher, or relative into the good or bad person, in contrast to his mother, so that he can wholeheartedly love and preserve the one, while all his angry, hating impulses are poured out on to the other. For instance, Dinah (2.9), at a time when she was feeling frustrated and angry with both her parents, turned away from them to a Miss P., who was living in the same house. She said to her mother one day: 'Miss P. is my best Mummy. She's my good Mummy, and you're my naughty Mummy.'

This suggests that there are other feelings involved in phantasies of attack besides anger and fear. Very early in his life a child feels grief at the damage he believes he has done, at his destruction of the bad, hated mother whom more and more he recognizes to be the same person as the good, loved mother. Although he may be shown repeatedly that in reality he has not harmed her and that she does come back, whole and loving, to feed and care for him, this is not always enough to convince him, for phantasy can be stronger than reality. Thus he suffers anxiety at the harm he may do, and grief and depression over the harm he feels he has done.

Paul (8) was legally put into his father's charge when his parents were divorced, as his mother was found to be unsuitable to look after him, although she was extremely affectionate towards him and he was devoted to her. The father remarried, but the new wife was a society woman who had no time for children, and arranged for Paul to go and live in the country with a governess, Miss R. Paul made a close and affectionate contact with Miss R., and often associated her directly with his own mother. When sitting with her by the fire in the evening, for instance, he would remember how he and his mother used to roast potatoes together, and once when looking at a photograph of his mother, remarked on how like her to look at Miss R. seemed to be growing.

One Christmas Paul's mother sent him a mouth-organ, which he had wanted for a long time. He played it continually and evidently prized it above all his other possessions, yet was extremely careless with it, resisting his governess's efforts to help him keep it safe. When eventually it was lost, Paul was filled with despair. More than ever the mouth-organ seemed to stand for everything that was good, and he was full of remorse for his carelessness, and said he felt he did not deserve to find it. At the same time he had a strong, half-voiced resentment against some unknown thief, hinting that he thought it was Martin, a cousin of the same age who was staying with them, and appearing to suspect Miss R. of being aware of Martin's guilt and of shielding him. Every day on returning from school, Paul asked her in an aggrieved way whether she had yet found his mouth-organ for him. He seemed unable to make a proper search for it, and wandered round the house in an aimless and depressed way, looking half-heartedly in the most unlikely places for it, even to the extent of digging in the garden in case it had got buried. Thus he missed the fact that it was all the time in the pocket of his best jacket, which hung by his bed. He became cold and distant towards Miss R., no longer going to her for a story at bedtime, or showing her things he had made. He also showed an unusual indifference and hostility towards her; for instance, he continually left his bedroom light on at all hours of the day, in spite of her reminders and requests to him to turn it off.

Some days after the loss of the mouth-organ, Miss R., who had taken on the work of Cub-mistress in the village, suggested to her Cubs that, as a good deed, they should all contribute money to buy Paul a new one. On being presented with it, Paul was deeply touched and almost speechless with gratitude. He said to Miss R.: 'I never thought that there would be such a kind person as you to think of such a thing!' He immediately became warm and affectionate to her again, and for the rest of the day played happily and actively. In the evening he sat with her by the fire and drew a picture for her which he asked her to put up on the wall, and he also pinned up two notices in his bedroom, one over his bed and one by the light switch, saying: 'Have you turned out the light?' and 'Wot—no electricity!' Before going to bed that night he made a complicated treasure box, with barricades and camouflage, in which to keep his new mouth-organ safe.

In this whole situation, which evidently held so much meaning for Paul, what seemed of special significance were his changes in feeling towards Miss R. Before the loss of the mouth-organ, he had tended to identify her with his mother as a good person; after the loss he seemed to see her as a bad mother-figure, grudging and hostile, while safely preserving the picture of his own mother, who had given him the mouth-organ, as a good figure. The bad Miss R. was felt not only to be unwilling to help him find the lost mouth-organ, but also to know where it was and to be with-holding it from him, as if she had never really wanted him to have it. He may have unconsciously felt that she kept it from him because he had stolen it in the first place, since Martin, the sus-pected thief, in general seemed to represent the aggressive part of Paul himself. They often did forbidden things together, Paul making the plans and directing the operations, but leaving any overtly aggressive act involved to be carried out by Martin. On the other hand, his suspicion that Martin was being shielded by her may have expressed a phantasy of the father and mother in league against him, Martin here standing for the father. In cutting him-self off from Miss R., Paul showed how dangerous she seemed, and how attacked by her he felt himself to be; at the same time, however, he was able to mourn for the lost mouth-organ as a good thing, willingly given to him by a loving mother and wan-tonly lost through his own carelessness. Paul's extreme happi-ness when he was given the new mouth-organ clearly sprang from relief at finding that Miss R. was after all friendly and helpful, and willing to let him have the thing he so much wanted. His remark 'I never thought that there would be such a kind person as you . . .' was perhaps another way of saying: 'You are still the good mother I used to think you were, and not after all the very bad mother you seemed to be.' The gift of a new mouth-organ must also have been a reassurance to Paul as to his own goodness and worth, on the strength of which he was able once more to love and actively create.

If one were to refer the words 'mouth-organ' literally to parts of the body, and to associate this idea with the fact that one sucks and blows a mouth-organ to produce a flow of music, one might see the episode as a dramatization of conflicting phantasies of a good mother who lovingly gives the child the breast, a greedy child who steals it from her, an unloving child who wastes it (as Paul wasted the electric light), an angry mother who withholds it in revenge for greed and theft, a sad and injured mother whose good breast is rejected, and a forgiving and still-loving mother who finally restores it. Many situations in later life which, in themselves, justifiably provoke sorrow and mourning, are coloured and intensified by the infant's grief over the good breast which he feels he loses through his attacks on it. Dinah showed this clearly during a period at the age of two years when she repeatedly dramatized situations in which attack and cruelty were followed by remorse and attempts to comfort and repair. She would throw her dolls on the floor, then immediately pick them up, saying: 'Poor dolly fall down. Dolly crying, dolly sad. I kiss her better. I want to make dolly better,' and one day, having angrily (and falsely) accused her mother of smacking her when she had wet her bed, she tried to open her dress, saying: 'Dear Mummy! Where are Mummy's buttons?' (her word for nipples) and 'Kiss Mummy's chest better.'

There is not always, however, the ability to mourn over destruction and loss, and, as in the case of Tony, there may be a strong denial of all painful feelings of grief. Tony's father was killed early in the war, and as his mother wanted to join the Forces when he was a baby of a few months old, she arranged for him to be looked after by a friend, who, when she became ill, handed him on to somebody else. At the age of five years he was so troublesome that his mother, who by this time had remarried and had another baby, was prevailed upon to take charge of him herself. She found Tony unmanageable: he hit and kicked her, took money from her purse, stole from shops, played truant from school, and stayed out in the streets for hours on end, so that she was only too thankful to take advantage of the evacuation scheme and send him to the country. At six years Tony showed that he was haunted by problems of destruction and loss for which he could find no solution. He could never allow himself to enjoy anything whole or unspoilt: a treat which he had looked forward to eagerly for days was always unsatisfying when at last it came, as for instance the pantomime, throughout which he repeated: 'It's all over now, isn't it? It didn't last long.' Sometimes he would appear to be trying to cheat himself out of what he wanted altogether, as when at the last minute he refused to get ready for the circus, as if determined to miss the train. Toys which he had longed for were broken or lost as soon as he had obtained them, or exchanged for something which, as Tony himself would point out, had no lasting value, such as a balloon or an ice-cream. He would sometimes accuse another child at school of having broken his new toy, or would insist that it was already damaged when he received it, blaming the shopkeeper or the person who had given it to him.

The same pattern was repeated again and again: as soon as the longed-for treat was over or the new toy broken, Tony would become full of aggressive activity, ruthlessly spoiling other people's work and damaging property, and seeking to make quarrels between other children or to get them into trouble. He generally blamed someone else for what had happened, but at the same time would make extravagant efforts to do something positive and useful in relation to some other situation, proudly inviting everyone to admire his handiwork, as if trying to convince himself of his constructiveness, and thereby deny the damage he had done. Such activities included doing services for his billet-mother without being asked, rearranging and redecorating his bedroom, endlessly building, 'bombing' and then rebuilding camps and huts in the garden, and doing jigsaw puzzles one after the other. He would pursue these tasks ruthlessly and aggressively until they were completed to his satisfaction, without regard for the wishes or needs of anyone else. It seemed as if he could not bear to face the thing he had broken or spoilt, perhaps because he felt convinced that nothing he had damaged could ever be mended or put right, and so, like Kay of the fairy tale as he sat in the Snow Queen's palace, endlessly trying to fit together the pieces of ice to make a whole, Tony tried to solve problems and to construct something in the outside world, without being able to deal with the problem inside himself. It is interesting to note that the episode of the ice puzzle was Tony's favourite part of the story of *The Snow Queen*: he would ask for it to be read to him several times, perhaps unconsciously recognizing that Kay's problem was similar to his own. In other ways, too, he was like Kay; for instance, he saw people mainly as hostile and unpleasant, as Kay did when his heart was pierced by the splinter of hate. Tony's failure to face his responsibility for causing people trouble and pain and his denial of their feelings might be paralleled by Kay's ruthless tearing-up of his grandmother's roses and his mockery of Gerda's grief over it, while the lack of basic contact with other people, which was so marked in Tony, could perhaps be seen to be symbolically expressed in Kay's leaving home and entering the frozen world of snow and ice, from which there seemed no escape.

One day when in trouble for wantonly breaking a piece of furniture, Tony likened himself to the Tin Woodman in the story *The Wizard of Oz* who could not feel because he had no heart, saying: 'You can break me up into pieces but you can't make me feel anything'; while on several occasions he asked, with satisfaction in his voice, what it was like to feel sorry for people. This determination to blind himself to the feelings of others and his refusal to acknowledge and mourn over the results of his own aggression suggest an underlying picture of himself as a dangerously destructive and essentially bad person, responsible at bottom for every misfortune that befell other people, so that to feel sorry for anyone ever would have been to confess to his own unlimited guilt. Such a phantasy must have been coloured for Tony by. the actual events of his life. Because his mother rejected him as an infant, and was not there in person to care for him, he never had the relief and reassurance of seeing that his early aggressive impulses towards her did not really harm her or make her hate him; her absence may well have been taken by him as proof that he had in fact been able to destroy her in his anger, while the subsequent rejections of him by the friends who looked after him, and finally by his mother again, can only have acted as further evidence that he was too bad to be tolerated or kept by anyone. In his desire to acquire material things—food, money, toys, and treats—and his subsequent behaviour towards them, Tony acted out repeatedly a pattern of wanting, having, damaging, and discarding, which perhaps to some extent illustrated his own experiences of being taken in and then thrown out. At the same time he seemed to be dramatizing the search for some good and satisfying thing which he longed to have, but felt unable to preserve and keep intact.

The prototype of this good thing which is sought throughout life is the breast. It is likely that the baby who is hungry and waiting to be fed at times feels that he creates something which satisfies and comforts him. Mike, at three weeks, grizzling as he lay waiting for food and restlessly turning his head from side to side in search of the breast, would suddenly stop still, transfixed as if by a vision, and remain thus for several seconds, his eyes tightly closed; he would then open them and burst into loud and angry cries, as if bitterly disappointed. On the basis of his feeding experiences, the baby feels he takes into him a good breast (mother), capable of living inside him, of loving him and giving him what he needs. This phantasy persists throughout life: at any age one may be comforted by warm and living images which are felt to be carried round inside one, or one can have a diffuse feeling of warmth and creativeness and life which seems to emanate from within; alternatively, at times there can be nothing but a cold, empty gap or a dead weight inside, with a feeling that all the goodness has gone out of life and nothing is worthwhile any longer.

In the case of Harry (3), the phantasy of a good mother-figure who could be kept safely inside him was dramatized in an imaginative game. Harry was the younger of two children; his father was a car dealer and spent much time away from home, and the mother, who was depressed, would periodically desert the children, with the result that they were left alone in the house for hours at a time. This happened on several occasions during Harry's first three years, until finally the mother did not return, and the children had to be boarded out and did not see her again. The father visited them spasmodically; he would promise to come on a certain day and impress on them that they must be ready for him at a particular time, but often he was hours late and sometimes did not come at all, which left Harry full of angry disappointment. Harry became closely attached to his foster-mother, and in his relationship with her lived through many phantasies which clearly originated in his feelings about his real parents. At times he could not let her out of his sight, and was miserable and angry if she had to go out without him, unable to accept her promise to return saying: 'You won't come back—you never do!' Here he seemed to have inside him the image of a bad mother-figure who was constantly in the state of deserting him, which was not allayed by the experience that his foster-mother did in fact come back to him each time. At other times, however, Harry would tell her when she was preparing to go out that *he* was going to take her for a ride in his sports car and, as she was leaving, would ask: 'Are you all right? Are you right inside?'

In the same way as when, feeling happy and loving and contented, the baby feels he takes in something actively good, loving, and satisfying, which he seeks to preserve and keep alive inside him, so when he is angry and frustrated he can feel that he takes in or has pushed into him (as he gulps and chokes over food that comes too late) something bad, injured, and revengeful, which hurts him from inside. An adult, falling asleep one night, was suddenly sharply awakened by the voice of her mother (who had died years before) saying in an irritated tone to her, as to a disobedient child: 'Come here!' She immediately felt convinced that the voice came from inside the bed, and a second later knew that it was inside herself. One day when Miss R. had been reading fairy stories to Paul and his cousin Martin, and they were discussing whether or not they believed in fairies, Martin said he believed that there were only two—a good one dressed in silver and a bad one in black, and that they made you happy or sad, at which Paul remarked: 'Yes, they're in your thoughts.' Miss R. said it sounded as if they might be inside you, and Paul added: 'Yes, the good ones eat the germs up, and the bad ones eat your blood.' The feeling that he has bad people and things inside him is a constant source of anxiety to the child lest they should attack from within and destroy both the things that he loves and values, and himself. There is therefore the need to project them into the external world, and this he feels able to do from his physical experiences of pushing things out of his body and making convulsive muscular movements—as in expelling urine and faeces, and vigorously kicking and screaming. Harry, in bed and saying goodnight to his foster-mother, repeatedly played a game in which he pretended to swallow her, saying triumphantly: 'Now you can't talk!' She had to be silent until he had ejected her (which he did with a realistic vomiting noise), at which he would immediately order her to start talking again. Perhaps he felt that it was not safe to keep her inside him for long as a bad person, that is, as someone who said bad things and so must be imprisoned and silenced (see page 69), while in her role as a good person who might be injured by greedy swallowing or made bad by being kept inside him, she had quickly to be restored, and must at once reassure Harry by the sound of her voice that she was still whole and unharmed, and not angry with him. Here Harry was testing the good and bad people he felt to be inside him in terms of an external person. One night he sat up late in bed, full of resentment because his foster-mother had promised to play with him, but had been detained elsewhere. When at last she appeared, Harry went straight to the lavatory, and on returning said with satisfaction: 'I've been sick!' His foster-mother asked what had made him sick, and he replied: 'Because I was so angry.' From the cheerful friendliness he then showed, it seemed as if he perhaps felt that, in being sick, he had successfully got rid of the bad, deserting mother who was persecuting him from inside, making him feel both angry and unwell, and could now make contact with the good one.

It seems possible that Paul in the episode of the mouth-organ was, among other things, dramatizing phantasies of what happened to the good breast-mother when she was taken inside him. The lost mouth-organ was all the time inside Paul's coat-pocket, near his bed, and, since clothes are so often felt to stand for their wearer, could thus represent an object inside Paul him-self. Because from one point of view it had become something bad by being stolen (in his phantasy) and lost, he forgot where he had put it, and did not think of looking in his pocket; in other words, he cut himself off from this bad thing inside him (ulti-mately, his own bad self), just as he cut himself off from the bad external mother, as represented by Miss R. The new mouth-organ, given him by a still-loving mother, was safely stowed away in a treasure box, where it had to be camouflaged and barri-caded against his aggressive impulses, and, from being cold, distant, apathetic, and restricted, Paul became warm and animated as if something had indeed come alive in him, and his thankfulness and genuine wish to restore led to a burst of creative activity.

In the course of normal development, children constantly equate projected inner figures with things in the reality world outside, and thereby not only experience relief from phantasies of internal attack, but reassurance in being able to measure and test their powers of destructiveness in terms of real things. It is in early infancy that this equation is normally made and the seeds of a relationship with reality are sown. When, as we have seen, the evil, persecuting breast (mother) is equated with the real mother who does not in fact torture and devour the baby, her bad aspects are modified, and can be taken inside him again as a less terrifying figure. When at a later age a child can project his own impulses to bite and to rush dangerously about in a noisy and uncontrolled way on to a barking, bounding dog, his actual experiences of a mild and friendly one help to modify not only his general impression of dogs, but also his picture of himself. This constant interaction of inner and outer worlds—the taking-in, pushing-out, and taking-in again of phantasy people and things—is the essence of growth in personality. Where, however, the child feels his aggression to be beyond all bounds, he may be paralysed with anxiety about the possibility of retributive attack, and so unable to make the equation between inner and outer objects, with the result that contact with reality is severely limited, and development comes to a standstill.

This was seen in the case of George, during the time when he was looked after by his grandmother, who was herself baulked and overwhelmed by his agggression, while at the same time his own mother was at the height of her anxiety over it. In these days George seemed to be shut into his own private world of violent persecution, from which he made very little contact with reality.

He did not play, but walked round the house looking tense and violent, sometimes muttering about 'air creatures' who dripped blood and seemed to be extremely dangerous. He was intensely suspicious of everyone, and carried many sharpened sticks as daggers in his belt, with which he would stab other children for no apparent reason. It was at this time that George was engrossed in his phantasies of Uncle Bill, and his grandmother said that his conversation bore little relation to anything that was actually happening around him.

Some months later George was moved into the care of Mr. and Mrs. B. Mr. B. was not only unafraid of George's aggression, but also helped him to control it by setting certain limits to it, and at the same time fostered his interest in things in the outside world. As a result of this help from a good father-figure, George became more able to express his phantasies in terms of real objects; for instance, instead of being preoccupied with 'air creatures' which, as figments of his imagination, could possess endless and immeasurably terrible powers, he began seriously to discuss such questions as: 'What would happen if you were mean to a lion?' In place of his rough daggers he started with Mr. B.'s help to make complicated swords and bows and arrows, which tended to serve him more as objects of self-adornment, and less as weapons with which to do actual damage.

In Roddy's case one saw how the changing character of his inner world was reflected in his behaviour and attitudes, while the experiences he had in the external world in their turn influenced his development as a person. Roddy went to a residential nursery school at the age of three years with his brother Patrick (2), having spent most of his second and third years in hospital suffering from various ailments, and having been neglected by his mother when he was with her. The parents were on bad terms with each other and there was a definite split in the family, the father preferring Roddy while the mother allied herself with

Patrick against them. She said that Roddy was not really her child, and in the morning, when the father had gone to work, would lock him out in the garden while she went back to bed with Patrick. Eventually she deserted both children and they had to be sent to the nursery school. When Roddy first arrived, he was an extremely backward and bewildered little boy, more like eighteen months in development than three years. He did not play, and was highly destructive; he could not speak, and indicated his wants by screaming. One of his chief problems, for which no physical cause had been found, was diarrhoea; he sometimes dirtied himself as often as twelve times a day, leaving a trail of excrement all over the house. He would also smear jam or honey over the floor, and would frequently take a work-basket, coal bucket, or box of toys, and scatter the entire contents in every direction. In these activities, as in the constant ejection of what must have seemed to him to be the contents of his own body, he was perhaps showing that he felt his inner world to be broken up into bits and therefore neither safe to keep nor worth keeping. At the same time he had a voracious and indiscriminate appetite: he would clap his hands with delight at the sight of food, would accept anything given him to eat, and would snatch everything within reach, stuffing it into his mouth as fast as he could, and always demanding more, however much he had had. Although Roddy showed little discrimination between one person and another and made few contacts with them, he disliked being left alone. In his attitude to his dirtying, too, he gave evidence of wanting to make a relationship with someone, for he would sing happily on the way up to the bathroom, and clearly enjoyed being cleaned up and changed, always refusing to try to help himself in any way, as by putting on his own clean trousers. He also showed an increasing delight in helping adults with household jobs—laying tables and clearing away after meals, washing up, wiping the floor, scrubbing potatoes, and even polishing the stairs.

As time went on, Roddy began to show a definite preference for the particular teacher who looked after him. When she sat in the garden sewing, he would bring a few toys and sit close by her. On one occasion he brought a spade, a cart, and four bricks, and proceeded to shovel the bricks on to the cart, laughing triumphantly and looking at her each time he succeeded in getting all the bricks on to the spade at once. In many other activities he showed a growing interest in amassing materials rather than in scattering them, in carting and heaping bricks, sand, and toys of all kinds, and pouring water from one vessel to another. At this point he still used materials indiscriminately, without regard for their real purpose; at a later stage he began to be more selective, sorting, grouping, and arranging objects, and rejecting those he did not want, and also showing definite likes and dislikes in relation to food. From his own teacher he demanded much more, wanting her in particular to do things for him. This developed into an insistence for a time that only she should do anything at all for him: he would lie in bed refusing to get up if anyone else called him, and although up till then used to sitting at meal-times at a separate table where he could have the full attention of a young member of staff, he began repeatedly to move all his cutlery to his teacher's table, laying it at the place next to hers, so that it had to be arranged for him to sit there permanently. Objects, too, became most important to him for themselves: he would insist on playing with one particular toy and that one alone; he would do a certain jigsaw puzzle over and over again; a special lavatory was *his* lavatory, and he would use no other one. By this time Roddy's dirtying had ceased: from defaecating anywhere and at any time he first began to have certain times, and generally to use the floor beside his pot; he then progressed to using the pot itself, and finally the lavatory, showing great satisfaction in his achievement. Roddy's pride in himself and his own property was shown in his frequent allusions to 'me' and 'my', and his repeated statements: 'My done this' and 'Me no like that.' He often sat up in bed gaily chanting: 'Noony, Noony, Noony's boy!' (Noony being his own particular name for his teacher), and was now so sure of himself that he could pretend to be something or someone else, such as a dog, or a train, or a 'daddy'.

It was clear that, from someone lost, bewildered, and in pieces, Roddy was building himself up into a whole and integrated person, with a strong conviction of his own identity. The fact that his diarrhoea as well as his other scattering activities gradually stopped at the same time as he himself became more constructive and purposeful suggested that he was coming to feel that the things inside him were no longer broken up into fragments, which had to be discarded, and one might feel that his amassing, piling up, and sorting of materials was representative of what was going on in his inner world. The very materials which before had stood for bad things that had to be thrown out of him now seemed to take on the meaning of good things that could be taken in and kept, this change probably occurring both because he became less afraid of the frightening things inside him through his contact with a good external mother-figure, and because he found himself able to construct and so could make them good. It is clear that this child's growth in personality was largely dependent on environment; at the same time, it was evident that something had grown up in him which could be independent of the outside, and which gave him a life and purpose of his own.

As the child's feelings become modified and his relationship with reality widens, the inner world of black and white grows less black and less white. But throughout his life he never loses his conception of the original good figures of his infancy, which in adulthood may be represented by constructive ideas, aims, and projects, and abstractions like truth and beauty, while bad figures can be felt still to exist in such forms as petty ambition, tyranny, and an unfulfilled contract. One of his chief concerns is to preserve inside him something good, and this ultimately depends upon his faith in his capacity to love, and his recognition and acceptance of his hatred.

CHAPTER TWO

The Influence of the Real World

ALTHOUGH, as we have seen, every child will inevitably have his phantasies, nevertheless they are very considerably influenced by what the real adults are like, and by the actual conditions of his life. There is constant interaction between the child's inner world of phantasy and the real external world, and it is through his increasing knowledge and experience of the outer world that his phantasy figures become modified, and he himself less at the mercy of them.

Perhaps we help children most in their development simply by being there; that is, by providing continuity and stability in their relationships. The effects of wartime evacuation have clearly demonstrated what separation from his parents and home can do to a child. In many cases children who stayed in the towns with their mothers and experienced the horrors of bombing and the irregular and unhealthy life of the shelters showed, both at the time and subsequently, that they were less disturbed and hindered in their development than others who grew up in peace and safety, but in homes to which they did not belong. The children who did manage to weather evacuation successfully were generally those who, on the strength of a stable relationship with their own parents, were able to make a sufficiently good contact with their foster-parents for the new home to represent the old, for the time being. The steady maintaining of close personal relationships is now recognized as essential for healthy development, and it is known that the child who has many breaks and changes in his early life, or is brought up in an institutional type of Home where individual attachments are not easily made, is apt to grow up into an unreliable and unsatisfactory person, often delinquent, with no power to make deep or lasting contacts with people, or to sustain any constructive purpose.[1] The personalities of these people are clearly the logical outcome of their experiences. Their phantasies of cruel, retributive parents who punish them by desertion must seem to be confirmed, while their pictures of themselves as omnipotently aggressive and destructive are not offset by the reassurance of an undestroyed family life, such fears and anxieties stifling their ability to love deeply, to experience grief, to make new contacts and to develop. Thus they grow up with their terrifying inner worlds unmodified, often seeking for something impossibly perfect, and with a deep feeling of disillusion and hopelessness as to their powers of making good. We have already seen something of this in the case of Tony, described in the last chapter, who never experienced stable family life, since his father died before he was born, his mother rejected him in his early infancy, and he was looked after by a series of mother-substitutes. By the age of six years he already seemed impervious to environmental help, for he was unable to form real attachments, and was interested in people only in terms of what they could give him, from a material point of view, setting so little value on them for themselves that he often muddled up the names and identities of those he knew quite well.

Will, aged thirteen, had a very different early background, for he and his sister were the children of a warm, affectionate, happy-go-lucky mother and an unreliable, ne'er-do-well father. Their first years were spent in wandering about the countryside with their parents, who made a livelihood in the summer by working in fairs and by poaching and stealing, and lived in workhouses during the winter. When Will was five and his sister three,

[1] See John Bowlby: *Forty-four Juvenile Thieves* (Baillière, Tindall & Cox).

the father was sent to prison and the mother died in childbirth. The two children were adopted by highly respectable relatives, who were shocked at their previous upbringing and determined to give them a new life, always living in fear lest they should follow in the footsteps of their parents. Will used at first to ask questions and talk openly about his parents and his life with them, but he was always answered negatively and told he must forget, and that he now had a new mother and father. Eventually he did seem to forget, but at great cost to himself. At thirteen he was an empty, limited boy who, although intelligent, did not fulfil his potentialities at school, and made no friends. He was shifty and evasive, telling lies, and engaging in persistent, solitary stealing, perhaps as a desperate attempt to keep his father alive, as well as in protest against his grudging and unsympathetic foster-parents. He was always polite and obedient and outwardly friendly, but he showed no spontaneity or purpose, even his stealing being aimless. Although, unlike Tony, Will was brought up by a loving mother until the age of five, and thus had the opportunity to form a good relationship in his early years, the fact that this did not stand him in good stead later must, in part, have been due to the violence and completeness of the break with his old life on which his adoptive parents insisted. In many cases, even where external circumstances necessitate the most irrevocable breaks in children's lives, they can be helped to keep alive in their own minds the relationships they have already made, and gradually, on the basis of these, to form new ones. This depends considerably on the substitute parents' willingness to preserve and strengthen every possible link with the past, and to give the child opportunity and encouragement to remember and talk about it, however unsatisfactory a past it may seem to them. If he can be helped to accept and build on his old external life, his inner life is less likely to be shattered. Harry, as we shall see later, deserted by his mother and neglected by his father, was able to make a new relationship in which he could work out problems relating to parents and family, and on the strength of which he continued to develop.

Whatever the circumstances of the break, if it is only for a few days or even hours, the important thing to a child is the keeping of home and parents alive inside himself. Children in nursery schools have often been soothed by such words as: 'Mummy's coming back soon; she's gone to buy the dinner', when all attempts to distract them had failed. The mother of Bobby, aged two years, had suddenly to go into hospital, where she remained for some weeks. Bobby was looked after by an aunt, who took care not to speak about his mother for fear of upsetting him. When the mother eventually returned home, Bobby treated her as a stranger and seemed terrified of her; he clung to his aunt, and it was some time before his mother could persuade him to go to her. Perhaps he felt that a mother who could not even be spoken of must be a very bad person indeed, while the fact that she seemed to have forgotten and completely abandoned him may have made him feel that she was angry with him, and that he himself was to blame for her going away, and had perhaps destroyed her for good. Thus as a bad, angry, destroyed mother, he could only fear her when she reappeared.

Separation from one or both parents can rouse intense feelings of deprivation, resentment, and guilt. But the parent who, although present in person, is absent in feeling—who is so deeply immersed in his or her own inner problems as to be detached from the child and oblivious of his needs and claims—can also be a source of deep anxiety, and may stultify the child's growth in personality. For instance, there is the emotional separation from the depressed mother, overwhelmed by gloom, passive and apathetic, yet strangely unreal to the child in the moments when she bubbles over with gaiety and excitement and is restlessly active. He is bewildered by her sudden changes in mood, and often unable to

cope with the implicit demand that he adjust his feelings to hers.
What we are and what we do affects children's development
in many ways. We can, for example, continue to reassure a
child that his harsh internal parents do not exist, or we can
bring them to life for him; we can also help him to build up a faith
in his own constructive powers and a confidence in himself, or we
can confirm his fears of being unable to make good the damage
he feels he has done. In the first place we can accept feelings of
anger and hate as an essential part of every normal child, and not
meet them with retribution or an injured, moral attitude. We
can allow him scope to test out his bad impulses, to see how far
he can go without causing external chaos and doing real harm.
One sometimes meets children who have never been allowed to
scream or have a temper tantrum, to dig in their heels and resist
authority, to shout out the angry things that come into their
heads, but have always been cajoled, distracted, or frightened
whenever they were on the verge of expressing strong feelings. A
teacher in a residential nursery school was known to pride herself
on the fact that the children in her group never got into tempers,
quarrelled with each other, or opposed her in any way, but were
always busy, creative, and co-operative. Because of their dependence on her they could only show the positive feelings which she
implicitly demanded from them, and so had no chance of discovering themselves as real people with bad as well as good
feelings, nor any way of telling how powerful and dangerous
these might be. Personality development, on such a basis, can
result in the adult who placates and apparently agrees with everyone, however violently their points of view conflict, continually
sacrificing his own convictions in order to avoid disagreement,
afraid of strong feelings both in others and himself. Often, however, at the same time he works steadily and subtly to make
trouble, for the urge to know how destructive bad feelings can
be is still there.

Fear of the child's aggression on the adult's part leads some-times to an inability to oppose him in any way, so that he finds himself in the frightening position of being able to rule her with his whims and tantrums. In such a situation he expects terrible revenge for his domination and exploitation of her, and these fears are not offset by real, mild control on her part. As a result, everyday situations tend to become unending dramas in which the child acts out his aggressive feelings over and over again, without gaining relief. The mother of Barry (4) was so fright-ened of 'scenes' that, having tried to cajole him into doing what she wanted, at the first hint of opposition she would give in and do almost anything to placate him. Her fear of what the neigh-bours would think if he screamed in temper forced her to read to him at 5.30 in the morning when he woke, and she would give up her morning's shopping or her afternoon's tennis if he said he wanted to stay at home. Barry was well aware of the power he had over his mother through her fear of his temper, and the fact that he himself was strained and anxious and could never let her out of his sight for a moment showed how guilty he felt at being able to dominate her so successfully, and worried as to the extent of the damage he could do to her. Clearly, it would have been a relief to him if she could have dared to be consistent and firm, and to face his anger when he did not get his own way.

In limiting aggression and destructiveness, it is necessary to take into account the meaning of the situation to the child him-self, as well as the claims of reality. One Christmas Day when Tony threatened to smash up his new train with a hammer, the person who was looking after him said: 'All right, it's yours: you can do what you like with it'—at which Tony proceeded to batter it to bits. The particular valuelessness of this experience to Tony was suggested some months later, when a rather similar situation was dealt with in a different way. Tony, in a fit of anger because he thought his billet-mother had given more foreign stamps to another child than to him, told her that he was not going to bother about stamp-collecting any more, but was going to leave his new stamp album (which had been his pride) out in the garden for the rain to spoil. When he went off to school, having carried out his threat, his billet-mother took the album to her room, to look after it until he felt better. As soon as he got back from school, Tony rushed straight out into the garden, and finding the album missing looked anxious and angry and unhappy, but said nothing. When his billet-mother showed him that it was safe, he was much relieved, and spent the evening happily sticking in stamps, and inviting her to admire each one as he put it in. On another day he told her that his own mother had a special white cupboard at home where she kept his toys 'all shining and tidy and not broken'—which, from all knowledge of his mother, was assuredly only wished for. It seemed as if the state of his train, his stamp-album, and his toys in the cupboard all represented to Tony his own condition and that of his inner world, and that when he got help from the adult to keep them safe and whole he had some proof that she felt him, as a person, worth preserving, and so was able himself to preserve and construct. As we have already discussed, Tony's usual pattern of behaviour was to destroy and then feverishly to mend and rebuild, only to destroy again. To feel happy and safe, a child must be able to find out where the limits lie: the adult who stands back and allows him to do exactly as he likes, refusing to stop him from doing harm, seems to be on the side of his worst impulses, and is often felt to be not only allowing, but aiding and abetting and ulti- mately even *causing* him to be 'naughty'. Many a child has turned to the adult and said: 'It's all your fault!' feeling that she should have stopped his bad behaviour before it reached such a pitch. This need for adult control was dramatized by Dinah (3) at a time when she was feeling angry and hostile towards her mother and new baby brother. She would pretend to be a wild animal, saying: 'I'm a very naughty tiger. I'm tempted to eat people up. I'm shutting myself up in a cage'; and, another time: ' I'm a Mrs. Pretend-lion. I'm a good lion. I don't eat people up because I've put myself in a cage.' Her mother was not allowed to pretend to be afraid, but was told: 'You're not frightened. You're the keeper.'

In the situation of the stamp album, Tony was helped by a measure of control on the adult's part, and by her support of the wish that lay behind his destructiveness, to make good and to preserve. In addition to this kind of help, a child also needs the opportunity to put angry and hostile feelings into words or dramatize them in his play, and to find that this is accepted by the adults. If, as in the case of Barry, the child's aggressive impulses are so feared by the adult that they can never be brought out directly, domestic life can become an intolerable battlefield in which phantasies of attack and counter-attack are constantly being acted out but never modified. Billy (3) was a timid, anxious child, unable to play freely or imaginatively, and limited in all his activities. His intense fear of his own aggressive wishes, and the persecution he felt from his surroundings as the result of them, have been mentioned already in Chapter I. Billy was obstinate and querulous in his behaviour over everyday domestic routine, and at bedtime especially would fly into a temper at the least frustration. One evening, when he was being bathed, he reacted to every move on his foster-mother's part with a temper tantrum, demanding one thing after another from her, and then angrily refusing it when it was offered to him. When it was time for him to be tucked up in bed, he was sobbing and shouting, hopelessly threatening : 'I'll tell my Mummy!' His foster-mother, having found that no amount of reassurance was any help, and feeling that Billy needed to be helped to express his hostility towards her more actively and openly, suggested to him that he must feel very angry with her, and would really like to shoot her, break her up, and burn her. Billy paused in his screams to listen. He then vigorously repeated several times that he was shooting her, with appropriate gestures, and proceeded to command her to 'get on the fire', asking: 'Are you all burning up?' Finally he summed up by saying: 'Broke you all up. You dead now. You on the fire. You all bleeding.' The foster-mother suggested that he might now want to mend her, which he pretended to do with eagerness, gently patting her and saying softly: 'Mend your arms, mend your nose, mend your eyes. Plaster on your arms, plaster on your back. You still bleeding? Oh dear!' This breaking-burning-shooting activity was repeated on many subsequent nights, followed by mending, re-breaking and re-mending, and always after it Billy was able to let his foster-mother say goodnight and leave him, with less anger and anxious calling her back than usual. It is seldom necessary actually to show a child how to put his aggressive feelings and wishes into words, as in the case of Billy; generally what is needed on the part of the adult is willingness to listen with tolerance, and a mild, unanxious response.

Caroline gained similar relief from becoming able to dramatize in her play feelings of hostility and aggression towards her mother. The mother was a smart and wealthy woman, who had a successful business and a beautiful house running smoothly and efficiently under her complete control. She evidently preferred the older child, Anthony (10), whose good behaviour and easy social manner fitted in with her standards; towards Caroline, who constantly made petulant scenes and behaved badly on public occasions, she was patient and sweet on the surface, but one could detect her underlying coldness and exasperation and basic lack of sympathy. There was clearly little affection between the two of them, and neither seemed to expect much from the other, apart from hostility and opposition.

For a short time during the school holidays, Caroline was looked after by a daily governess, whom both she and her mother were inclined to treat in an arrogant and domineering manner. Caroline tried to control her in every possible way: for instance, she could not willingly allow her to go to the lavatory, but would kick angrily on the door, shouting through the keyhole: 'Hurry up! You've been there long enough! You must come out at once!' When the governess read to her, Caroline would constantly interrupt to make her start again at a different point in the book, and when they went to the Zoo together, the least indication of interest in anything on the governess's part brought about anger on Caroline's part, and insistence that they should immediately go and see something else. In the garden she would play over and over again a game in which the governess, as the baby, had to keep waking up after being put to bed, and call for mother. Caroline, as the mother, varied in her responses between running anxiously to the bedside saying: 'There, there, darling! Mummy will bring you a sweet', and refusing to come at all, shouting angrily from the other end of the garden: 'Go to sleep, you horrid little beast!' Another game, centring in her doll Milly, involved the lengthy preparation of many birthday presents and a wonderful cake, and the dressing of Milly in her best clothes, with much endearment. Inevitably, however, Milly was made to commit an offence—her arm would not go into her dress, or she was said to have thrown a plate out of the window—at which she was immediately stripped of her party clothes, beaten, and sent to bed, and the teddy bear was given her place at the birthday party, and pampered and praised in front of her; as Caroline once triumphantly remarked: 'She *thought* she was going to have *her* birthday, didn't she!'

In these play situations Caroline seemed to be dramatizing a phantasy of a mother whose harshness was the inevitable response to a child so wicked that she should never have been born—in so far as her very birthday had to be taken away from her. In her triumphant condemnation of the naughtiness of Milly and her satisfaction when she was punished, Caroline was surely confessing her own guilt and insisting on her own need for punishment. It is clear that the behaviour of the real mother, although far less harsh, coloured rather than modified the phantasy of the cruel, retributive mother Caroline felt she deserved, and that her need was for a mild mother-figure who could tolerate displays of hostile and aggressive activity without herself becoming hostile and reacting aggressively, a role which, for the time being, the governess was able to fill. Caroline's first tentative and spasmodic attempts at imaginative play were followed by a rapid increase in confidence and richness of expression when she found that she could play freely without criticism or disapproval, and could enlist the governess's active participation when she needed it. The play itself was never modified during the few weeks that the governess was there, but the more violent it became—the naughtier the child, the angrier the mother, the harsher the punishments—the more peacefully Caroline herself seemed able to co-operate with her governess, to trust her, and to show the first faint signs of affection for her. Her sharp expression began to soften, her voice grew a little less shrill and querulous, and her whole attitude seemed gentler, and alongside these changes there was an evident increase in her sense of reality. One day, after playing through once again the episode in which Milly was whipped and starved for throwing plates out of the window, Caroline said to the governess: 'What would you do to me if I really threw a plate out?' When asked what she thought, she replied: 'Make me go and pick it up.'

To advocate mildness and tolerance does not imply that the adults who are the best for children never show negative feelings, but suppress every trace of anger, disappointment, and grief, and appear to them as invulnerable and imperturbable. Children need to grow up among real people who feel deeply, but who show that it is generally possible to deal with their feelings, and to carry on without being overwhelmed by them. The mother who never dares to be angry with the children, but struggles always to be mild, patient, and forbearing under the utmost provocation, may make them anxious and over-dependent on her. They never have the relief of finding out that she can be angry without becoming dangerous, nor the experience of discovering that both her feelings and theirs can be expressed without doing permanent harm. Guilt about feeling angry with a mother who is herself never angry, and fear lest he should hurt her, may make a child wretchedly bound to her; he may feel that he should give her everything, and never be able to leave her in order to do anything on his own. Frank outbursts on the adults' part which are quickly over may sometimes be of value to children; on the other hand one knows that the more insidious adult ways of expressing feelings, nagging, for instance, bitter sarcasm, or an air of martyrdom, can only make for resentment and anxiety.

It is not difficult to reconcile tolerance with spontaneous shows of feeling on the part of the adults if we act on intuitive understanding of what different situations mean to an individual child. There are many everyday occasions when his feelings are not deeply involved, and we can let him know frankly, in words if possible, that we feel annoyed or worried or disappointed on account of something he has done. There are other situations in which, if we have a sympathetic contact with the child, we shall realize that his anger, anxiety, or disappointment is great, and so will not react solely to the trouble he has caused. In other words there is little place for conscious patience, which generally implies an underlying impatience and intolerance, and lack of appreciation of the child's point of view. Children are quick to feel the difference between patience and real acceptance. In certain situations where the adults are annoyed or upset for reasons of their own which in the first place have nothing to do with the children's behaviour, it can sometimes be reassuring to give some explanation of this. It is not always possible to hide feelings successfully from children, and efforts to do so can at times give them an impression of falsity and unnaturalness, or can create anxiety and tension arising from fear of feelings so dangerous that they must be concealed, and something in the air too dreadful to be spoken of. In such a situation a child may also feel guilty, unconsciously suspecting that it is his own aggressive impulses that have taken effect, and in his anxiety may react with difficult behaviour, thus giving himself evidence that it is indeed he who is causing the trouble.

One important fact which it is essential to recognize is the child's very deep need to repair the damage that he feels he has done. If he can be given time to face the fact that his own angry, hating impulses have caused harm, and to feel sorry in his own way, he will gain from the situation, especially if he is given the opportunity to make reparation. Roddy showed how a situation of attack, grief, and reparation can be lived through, and how the full experience can add depth to personality. When he and his younger brother, Patrick, first came to the residential nursery school at the ages of three and two years, one of the most striking things about them was their extreme hatred of each other: they could not bear even to be in the same room together; they quarrelled on almost every possible occasion, and each would scream angrily whenever the other one was getting the attention of an adult. Although, as we have seen, Roddy improved in nearly every way, his relationship with Patrick did not change much during those first few months. He was almost always submissive towards his younger brother, giving in completely to his demands and tyranny: if Patrick wanted something Roddy was using, he had only to hit him or even threaten to do so for Roddy to give up the object without resistance, and to run behind an adult, crying with fear. Occasionally Roddy would attack Patrick in a furtive manner, as when, meeting him in a dark passage, he hit him on the head with a book, but generally he would go out of his way to avoid violence. On the other hand, Roddy was most anxious for the adults to control Patrick, and would often point out his misdemeanours with an indignant and triumphant expression. Their dislike of each other was matched by their mutual dislike of cats: whenever either Roddy or Patrick passed a cat they would kick or hit it, and if they saw one in the distance they would often make threatening gestures and angry noises at it. When a cat approached them they would scream with fear, and Roddy, on several occasions, became quite frantic when he found one asleep on his bed.

One night when Roddy's particular teacher was away, a little ginger kitten belonging to her was found dead outside her bedroom door, with its head crushed in. Roddy's bed was close to the cupboard where the mother cat had just moved the kitten, and he was known to have been out of bed several times that night, whereas all the other children were asleep. Some weeks later when Roddy was in the garden on his own for a few minutes, he was seen to attack another kitten of a previous litter, stamping on it so hard that it became almost unconscious. Roddy's teacher rescued it, and then took Roddy into her room and confronted him with the kitten, wrapped in a blanket, lying on the sofa. She said: 'Look, Roddy, look at poor Sandy: Sandy's got a bad bump.' Roddy began to cry in a most upset way. She said: 'Who hurt him?' and Roddy, with tears streaming down his face, pointed to himself, saying: 'Me.' The teacher then said 'Poor Sandy! How can we make him better?' Roddy stroked the cat gingerly; she repeated the question and he kissed it, and also kissed his teacher and clung to her and stroked her, as if wanting to comfort and be comforted. As soon as she stopped expressing sorrow for the cat, Roddy became noisy and over-cheerful, but he quietened down again when he saw that she did not respond. He went off to play, and was soon rushing round the house in a wildly excited manner, shouting at the top of his voice and running from person to person showing them things, except when he came into contact with his own teacher, when he became subdued and quiet again. At dinner time he sat beside her silently, unable to eat. When he passed a cat in the passage, he said: 'Aah!' endearingly, as he did when being loving to his teacher; several times he climbed on to her knee and sat there thoughtfully, stroking her. Later in the day he fell down and bumped his head quite severely. By night time the kitten had recovered, as it had only been suffering from shock, and when Roddy's teacher went to say goodnight to him, she took it with her. Roddy seemed pleased, and stroked and petted it, and then suddenly pointed to his own head and to the kitten's, saying triumphantly: 'Two bumps!' This he repeated for days afterwards, whenever he saw the kitten. From that moment Roddy showed a great affection for cats in general, and for Sandy in particular; he began to claim him as *his* cat, tried to entice him into his bed, and loved to stroke and cuddle him. When Sandy jumped on to the table and stole food, Roddy would remove him gently, with a shocked expression.

It seems likely that Roddy's hatred of cats was due very considerably to his jealous feelings towards them in relation to his teacher, that he saw them as rivals, and that they stood among other things for his brother Patrick. He feared them because he expected them to attack him in response to his own wish to attack them. He also showed that, in his mind, the kitten represented not only Patrick, but his teacher and himself as well: in injuring the kitten he felt he had injured her, and so needed to stroke and try to comfort her; at the same time, he felt that he himself had been injured, as he showed by seeking comfort and later by bumping his head. When he was brought face to face with the results of his aggression towards Sandy, Roddy accepted his guilt and felt real grief and a wish to make him better, and loving feelings replaced hate. In his teacher's presence he could not keep up his attempt to escape from painful depression by wildly rushing about, and perhaps was more able to face his grief when she was there to help him. In bumping his own head, it seems that Roddy might have felt he was atoning for Sandy's injury by punishing himself and sharing the cat's pain; it was clear from the satisfied way in which he exclaimed: 'Two bumps!' that it was a positive thing to him. His pleasure in becoming able, at the last, to identify fully with the cat might also point to the fact that all along it had stood for Roddy himself, as the down-trodden, badly treated brother. In representing himself simultaneously as a cruel, attacking child, he was perhaps giving the reason for this ill-treatment. The problem was lessened when the teacher not only restored the injured child and demonstrated her love for him, but also showed she did not reject the naughty child, and instead helped him to become someone who could himself love and restore.

The value of this experience to Roddy, which might have been a disastrous one making him more afraid than ever of his aggressive impulses, lay in the opportunity he had to mend and make good, and also in the fact that he was led to face his own feelings of guilt and grief. It now seems certain that this important experience contributed to Roddy's ability to stand up to his younger brother, to face Patrick's violence and uphold his own rights, and at the same time to feel the beginnings of an affection for him. Gradually they became able to co-operate in their play and to share possessions: they began to greet each other lovingly when they had been parted, and to stand up for one another against the other children. Patrick went through a phase in which he called Roddy 'Daddy', and continually asked for his help in such matters as undoing buttons or manipulating a toy, which Roddy always gave delightedly. When Roddy heard Patrick crying, he would look anxious and run to see what was the matter; when Roddy was in bed with a cold, Patrick was con-tinually going upstairs 'to see my big brudder'. Although they still quarrelled, the tension between them, which both had found so intolerable, had gone.

Much could be said about the meaning of the original family situation to Roddy and Patrick, and their resulting feelings about each other. One aspect of their changed relationship might be that, with the reinstatement of Roddy as a real older brother with rights of his own and a strong personality, who could be kind and helpful as well as controlling and dominating, Patrick was no longer at the mercy of phantasies of a brother who was cruel and hating and might one day rise up and pay him back for stealing the mother and keeping her all to himself, and who must therefore be constantly attacked and kept in subjugation. On the other hand, Roddy found that it was safe to stand up for himself and to show his strength without destroying Patrick as he perhaps had feared, and also that he could do positive and good things to him, through being bigger and stronger.

When, on the spur of the moment, Roddy's teacher had to deal with the situation of the cat, she did not realize the full sig-nificance of it, and it was not until later that she understood more of what it meant to him. At the time, she saw it simply as a situa-tion in which Roddy's essential need was an opportunity to make reparation, and at the same time to face and not escape from his feelings of grief. An attitude on the part of the adults which helps a child to live through a difficult situation and to find some sort of solution does not always demand full understanding of the meaning of it; what is needed primarily is appreciation of the fact that these things do mean a great deal to children, and that beneath acts of violence and destruction there is inevitably anxiety and a longing to be able to put matters right, however unlikely this looks on the face of things.

There are many situations in childhood in which deep and

complex feelings are involved which cannot always be understood at the time, but can be handled and accepted in an understanding way. The arrival of a new baby is an event which is always meaningful and disturbing to a child, even if he appears unmoved by it or expresses only positive feelings towards it, and at such a time he particularly needs sympathy and help, and sometimes tolerance of unusual or difficult behaviour. One saw this clearly in the case of Harry, who was very much upset when his foster-mother took another child into her home. When Harry first came to her at the age of two years with his older sister Joan, he was a miserable, undernourished little boy who was markedly backward. He quickly became attached to his foster-mother and became secure and happy as the baby of the household, growing independent, and playing constructively and imaginatively both on his own and with neighbouring children. The foster-mother told Harry and Joan well beforehand that a little boy, Billy, was coming, explaining that although he was two years old, he was very small for his age and could barely walk and talk, and so seemed more like a baby and would need much care. The day before his arrival, when she was discussing it with the children, Harry said: 'I'm going to read *That Baby*'—a book about a small boy's jealousy of his baby brother and the mother's efforts to help him. He identified himself at once with the older boy, showed disgust at a picture of the baby eating messily, and enthusiastically accepted the suggestion of the boy next door that in one picture the older child was about to throw the baby on the fire. In this way he showed some awareness of what the event was going to mean to him.

Harry's reactions to Billy were violent, and his variable behaviour and the many contrasting attitudes he took up in relation to him and to his foster-mother revealed vivid phantasies and much conflict of feeling. From the first day, he showed sudden loss of independence and reversion to babyish habits. He became 'unable' to eat his food, asking for something and then having to leave it, and began to eat in a messy way, crumbling his food up and stuffing it into his mouth with both hands. On two occasions he dirtied himself, a most unusual occurrence, and also started wetting his bed at rest-time, which he had not done for several months. One evening he sat on his foster-mother's knee whimpering that he could not walk to bed and would have to be carried; he also sometimes insisted on being put to bed before Billy and would refuse to dress himself in the morning, asking for help where before he had managed on his own. Instead of playing happily and independently, as he used to do, he would wander round the house in an aimless way, continually seeking out his foster-mother to make some complaint and gain comfort. Harry dramatized and summed up this situation on several successive nights in the bath, holding long duologues with a celluloid fish in which he was the father, gruff and sensible, and the fish was a querulous little boy with a high-pitched voice who repeatedly protested that he could not do what the father wanted: for instance, one night the father told the fish to shut its mouth, and the fish whined persistently that it was not able to.

The deep distress that Harry felt at the coming of Billy was clear. For many nights he woke crying, complaining of a pain, a headache, a sore face or nose, or a hurt leg. On the day Billy arrived, he silently buried his face in his hands several times as if crying, and when he returned that evening after a ride in his father's sports car, he lay on the floor, heaving as if with sobs, and could not be moved. He would cry at the least setback, and frequently imagined that he was being attacked or insulted, reacting with angry tears. He was always falling down, and day after day cut his knees open, often blaming another child. With his crying, his physical injuries, and his helplessness, Harry claimed much attention and comfort from his foster-mother. At the same time he showed great hostility to her: he refused to do almost everything she asked him to, but showed no satisfaction in resisting her, generally crying anxiously; when reprimanded he was abject, but would repeat the same act shortly afterwards. He broke things, told lies, and was particularly defiant and disobedient over matters of domestic routine which he had formerly accepted without question.

Towards Billy himself, Harry showed comparatively little hostility. On the first day, when he was hit by him, he complained bitterly to his foster-mother and cried; when Billy continued to hit him, he eventually hit him back gingerly, saying: 'I don't like that boy; he's a naughty boy; he's not allowed to hit people; he's got a dirty face; he's not nice.' He evidently feared the effect that retaliation on his part might have. In general he showed that he was afraid as to what his hostile impulses might do to him; perhaps it was for this reason that he would come in from the garden to ask: 'Is Billy all right?' He also seemed very much afraid of Billy's aggression, and felt constantly attacked by him, often complaining without justification that he spoilt his games. One morning he and Tommy, the boy from next door, locked themselves in a room for several hours to play, as if feeling the need for protection from Billy.

On this and many other occasions Harry seemed to be trying to make an alliance with Tommy against the foster-mother and baby: he played regularly with him, offered to let him share his possessions, and even addressed him on one occasion as his brother—'because', he said, 'you love me'. At the same time he seemed to be dramatizing and testing out in relation to him feelings that really belonged to Billy, for he found many ways of persecuting him, frequently hitting him and telling tales in order to get him into trouble. It was possibly because his fears of the disastrous consequences of his aggression were so great that he was not able to attack the real object of his hostility, but instead chose people who could defend themselves against him. At mealtimes

47

he frequently hit Joan, his next-door neighbour, complaining that she was attacking him, and went out of his way to quarrel with her, but said: 'I like sitting next to Joan', as if he found her a convenient person on whom to vent his angry feelings. Not only did Harry show little direct hostility to Billy, but he also made considerable attempts to establish a good relationship with him, and on many occasions initiated games with him. As time went on he showed increasing tolerance of his tiresomeness and would correct or reprimand him mildly, calling him a 'little scallywag', and wanting to deal with his accidents and mistakes, to mop up and tidy up after him. He sometimes protected him against dangers, real or imagined, and was indignant when Joan tried to supervise or take care of him. He showed interest in his development, would encourage him with the words: 'Clebber boy!' and often commented wisely on his achievements to his foster-mother. Eventually these earnest efforts to love Billy gave way to a more casual attitude to him, and Harry's feelings of persecution and acute rivalry abated, and he became able once more to be independent and to play happily and constructively.

It seems likely that Harry's ability to get through this very difficult and painful situation was at least partly due to his foster-mother's help. The state of misery to which he was so easily reduced showed how deserted and neglected he felt himself to be, imagining as he did that she had transferred all her love to Billy, and his symptoms were clearly a call for help and comfort. At the same time his aches and pains showed how much he felt attacked from within as well as from without, and his dirtying and wetting, his tears and complaints, must surely have in part symbolized to him his intolerable feelings of anger and jealousy which he had to get rid of. Above all, he needed his foster-mother to stand by him and bear his anger and jealousy; he was also helped by her showing him, sometimes in words and sometimes in actions, that she knew something of his feelings and realized that he was in considerable difficulty. On many occasions she told him that she knew he was afraid that she no longer loved him, now that she had Billy, and also related his aches and pains to angry and uncomfortable feelings inside him, although always, at the same time, accepting physical symptoms at face value, and giving him the cold cream, plaster, or breakfast in bed that he seemed to feel he needed.

Although this situation was for Harry most painful and upsetting, the fact that the living through of it with help was important to him in his development was shown by the striking increase, during the months following his recovery, in his ability to express phantasies. These in themselves became richer and more varied, and he found relief in his added power to verbalize his feelings. In Harry's case, as in general, it was better that he was able to face and express his grief and anger than that he should deny them, or simply never care, and in view of the fact that he had been, in reality, deserted by his mother, it was particularly valuable to him to experience such feelings in relation to a substitute.

One of Harry's chief problems in this particular situation was the conflict between wanting to grow up and to remain a baby. It is sometimes thought that growing-up means for a child the giving up of pleasure and the taking on of unwelcome responsibility, and that he painfully struggles to acquire self-control and to behave sociably mainly in order to keep his parents' love and approval. Growing-up, however, means far more than this: it is one of the child's greatest reassurances against his fears of his own destructive impulses. Learning to walk and talk and be clean, to read and to write, are proofs to him that he can be constructive, and help to offset his phantasies of destroying and spoiling. Perhaps one of our main ways of helping children to develop happily and successfully is by encouraging them to be active and practical, to make and do, to experiment and find out, to collect and care for. The intense satisfaction young children experience in becoming independent and in doing positive, concrete things points to the fact that, in general, all normal children want to grow up. Malcolm, the younger of two, was unusually helpless for a boy of five and a half years, although not unintelligent. His mother generally combed his hair, cleaned his teeth, fastened his shoes, and cut up his food for him; he could not feed himself without covering his face, clothes, and the tablecloth with food, and usually dropped or spilt anything he had to carry. Malcolm's mother made it clear that she did not believe him to be capable of doing any of these things for himself, and Malcolm, when he did not get what he wanted done for him at once, would shout angrily: 'I'm only a very little boy!' One afternoon when his mother was out, the friend who was looking after him casually asked him to boil an egg to make sandwiches for tea. Malcolm was delighted, and carried out the exploit quite competently, later describing to everyone in detail exactly how he had boiled it. When his mother came home, he shouted triumphantly: 'I've been cooking—all by myself! I know how to do it!' On that one afternoon, at least, Malcolm experienced the positive value and pleasure of being capable, independent, and grown-up.

Why did Peter Pan not want to grow up? Why did he prefer to remain an irresponsible, unreal sort of child, living in an unreal world from which he sometimes gazed wistfully at the real world of children and parents? One might see this fairy story as a vivid dramatization of a phantasy common among children. When Peter Pan flew back home after living with the fairies, he found that the nursery window was barred and his mother had another little boy in his place. His experience of the adult world was one of unfaithfulness and inconstancy, and he became bitter and mocking in his attitude to adults, and determined not to grow up to be a man. His mother could not accept his changing feelings—his whim to fly away from her, and later his longing to return—

and shut him out as a punishment for his wanting to leave her, replacing him with another child. Perhaps it was the lack of a mother who would stand by him and accept his feelings that led Peter Pan to escape from his own responsibility and guilt, to push all the blame on to the grown-ups, and to assume a false kind of airy joyfulness. Mothers were silly and unnecessary, he said; and yet he often returned to the world of ordinary parents and children to hide in eaves of houses, and watch and listen.

It seems then that, although a child's mind is not a mirror faithfully reflecting what goes on outside him, his experiences and particularly his relationships with the adults in his world do matter to him. Through affection and mild, understanding control and contact with genuine people, a child can be helped to see himself and the people and things around him less in the extreme black-and-white terms of phantasy, and to be a real person with feelings of which he is not afraid.

CHAPTER THREE

The Mouth as a Centre of Feeling

No one who has seen a tiny baby being fed can doubt that sucking is of the greatest importance to him: not only is it his means of physical survival, but also the centre of his emotional life. As with his mouth the baby makes an active contact with his mother's breast, he has his first experiences of the give-and-take of a human relationship, and of the gratifications and frustrations of the outside world. There must be some moments when he is aware of it as an object apart from himself, and others when he feels at one with it, in a phantasy of incorporating it or extending himself into it.

This earliest relationship is, to some extent, the pattern for every other relationship in life. For instance, it underlies the pupil–teacher relationship, in which willingness and ability to give something good is matched by eagerness to take in what is offered and to see it as 'good'—to 'lap up' or 'drink in' information and to be 'hungry for knowledge'—while, conversely, the teacher who 'stuffs facts down one's throat', 'spoon-feeds', expects one to 'swallow everything whole', and gives one 'mental indigestion' and no time to 'chew over' questions is likely to complain that his pupil 'won't take anything in' and 'can't get his teeth into the work', and that the material he provides 'goes in at one ear and straight out of the other'. We see something of this pattern, too, in talking and listening relationships: the very images we use to illustrate what we feel about speech and its functions are often phrases which really express ideas about food and feeding.

We speak of 'honeyed' and 'soothing' words, of 'bitter', 'acid', and 'biting' remarks, and of someone who 'never minces his words', while one person 'nearly snaps one's head off', and another 'forces one's words back down one's throat'. Many attitudes in later life may be seen to be based on feelings belonging to the early feeding relationship, as, for instance, that of the dominating, highly possessive woman who seems to devour her husband and children; the over-fastidious, unsatisfied man who rejects everything in a lifelong search for something perfect and unfailing; the impatient, anxious person for whom everything always comes too late to be of any value; and the placid, contented person who 'takes things as they come', and seems able to make the best of any situation.

Throughout life, too, the mouth itself remains important as a centre and means of expressing feeling, and the actual pleasures of sucking, biting, and taking into oneself are repeated at every age and stage, not simply in relation to food, but in the making and experiencing of relationships. Christopher, at two, played biting and sucking games of all kinds with his mother, who seemed to enjoy them almost as much as he did; another mother said that she loved her child so much that she could eat him, while yet another would clench and grind her teeth with intense pleasure whenever she played with the baby. In adult sexual life, a pretence at biting is often a form of endearment, while kissing is surely a recapitulation of the earliest delights of making contact and gaining sensations through the mouth.

We know, from the work referred to on page 2, that the child's earliest phantasies originate in the feeding situation, and that these endure throughout life, and are repeatedly re-lived in later situations. For instance, the baby's phantasy that in taking milk from the mother he takes her inside him, preserves her, perpetuates her goodness, and makes her part of himself, reappeared in Harry's wish to feel able to keep his foster-mother safely inside his sports car (himself) when she went out; it is shown in the attempts by young children to swallow treasured possessions, and in the adult's sensation at times that he is overflowing with warm, loving feelings, and has a comforting and satisfying object inside him (sometimes indentified as the heart) which is the source of all goodness. The need to make sure that the good object is benefited by being taken inside was illustrated by Dinah, who would ask whether the food she ate liked to be eaten. When she was 2.8, the following conversation took place:

Dinah: 'Does the cow like the milkman lady to take away the milk?'

Mother: 'Yes, because she has too much, and she would be uncomfy.'

Dinah (her face lighting up): 'She would be sick!'

After this she would say: 'The milk likes to be drunk up in my tummy because it's nice and warm there.'

This conversation also points to the fact that there is anxiety lest when food is taken from the good-mother she should be robbed of all her goodness, and left empty, exhausted, and destroyed. This infantile phantasy is seen to persist in the confused idea sometimes held by children that their own growth in some way involves taking vital material from their parents, thus impoverishing them, and they talk about a time 'when I'm big and Mummy's little'. Dinah, at three years, had her own theory of 'growing up' and 'growing down', which will be discussed more fully later. One day she said to her mother: 'When I'm a big lady, Jim will be a big man, and he can be my wife and help me shell peas. You will be a tiny baby then, and Jim will be your daddy'—Jim being a three-and-a-half-year-old cousin. In the same way she described how when Libberbel, her baby doll, was grown-up, she herself would become the tiny baby. An adolescent girl will sometimes feel unduly anxious about the natural ageing of her mother, as if it were her fault and perhaps due to her own increase in attractiveness, and may unconsciously fear retaliation from her—a fear which at base is the infantile fear of retribution by the breast that has been robbed and made dangerous and hostile. This phantasy is dramatized in the fairy story of *Snow White*, in which as the child increases in beauty, the queen, feeling robbed and displaced, becomes angry and full of wish for revenge, until eventually, in the guise of a wrinkled old woman, she tricks Snow White into eating the poisoned apple. Such fears of taking from the mother underlie and are in part responsible for the many feeding problems seen in childhood and later life, as we shall see vividly in the cases of Peter, George, and Lionel.

Attempted defences against greed and its results may also lead to general personality problems, as for instance in the woman who can never allow anyone to help her in the house, but has a self-righteous satisfaction in making a slave of herself and persuading everyone else to exploit her, in order to try to atone for the greed and exploitation inherent in her own infantile phantasies. She herself is becoming the exhausted mother whose energy and goodness are greedily dragged out of her by the child, now represented by her own family. The same phantasy seems to operate in the person who cannot acknowledge his own success and is ashamed when congratulated, and also in someone who is unable to enjoy a gift, having always to accuse the donor of extravagance. Such people seem deeply convinced of their own unworthiness, their inability to take without harming, much less to do good by taking. To them, indifference and rejection are the only safe measures: to accept would mean not only to grasp greedily, thereby robbing someone else, but to become possessed of something essentially dangerous, which would assuredly 'bite back'. Another aspect of the attacked and angry breast is that of its retaliation by withholding or by giving grudgingly—a phantasy which may prompt people, at all stages of life, to demand and snatch whenever the opportunity arises. In such a person there is often the feeling that he has lost the good thing he most needs, and, like Tony, he may go through life empty and unsatisfied, looking in the outside world for what he really lacks inside, and grabbing and tasting everything, only to throw it aside as worthless. There can also be a phantasy of a cold, dead, indifferent breast which has been killed by the baby's greedy onslaughts, and may, as already suggested, be felt almost physically as a cold, empty, aching space inside.

In the case of Lionel, a specific feeding problem seemed to arise from the need to reject food because it had been obtained by exploitation of the mother. Lionel was an intelligent boy of four years who lived alone with his mother, his father having been killed in the war. His mother idolized him, frequently commenting on the fact that he was the image of his father, and talking about him in an admiring way in front of him. She was unduly concerned over his welfare, always worrying as to whether this or that would 'suit' him, and Lionel fully exploited this anxiety, making many demands on her, opposing every wish of hers, and usually getting his own way by crying. When he was with his mother, he ate practically nothing, and she was so worried lest he should lose weight that she would prepare food for him at any time of the day or night, however inconvenient to her, trying, as she said, 'to tempt his appetite'. Lionel would often wake in the night and rouse her to make him sandwiches and a hot drink, while throughout the day he would demand little titbits. He was always asked to choose what he would like for the next meal, but showed no satisfaction at having his wishes fulfilled, appearing anxious whenever his mother went into the kitchen to cook what he had chosen, hanging round her whining, and eventually, when it was offered to him, refusing to eat it. His anxiety disappeared when, for a while, he was looked after by a friend who was unconcerned about his eating, and he ate normally and with enjoyment, but again began to refuse food of all kinds as soon as his mother returned. What stood out clearly was the fact that the mother's almost slavish devotion to Lionel's wishes and her refusal ever to oppose him in any way increased his anxiety, and so intensified his resistance and his inability to eat. This anxiety must have sprung from a feeling that, since his mother really did suffer from his exploitation of her, his aggressive wishes towards her were fully taking effect. Perhaps also there was an underlying feeling that food which had been obtained at her expense could not be eatable.

Such phantasies of a mutually persecutory relationship, which originate in very early days when the child is at the sucking stage, are considerably intensified when he begins to bite. At a few months, he enjoys playing with his gums on his mother's nipple in a loving way, but when he is angry and frustrated this can also be felt to be a way of attacking her, bringing phantasies of a bitten-up, destroyed breast (mother), and of a something in pieces which angrily attacks him from inside, perhaps by producing 'gnawing' colic pains, screams which seem to tear him to pieces, or the soreness of his gums when he is cutting his teeth. At weaning time, the baby's natural enjoyment of biting may be tempered by the phantasy that he is being punished for having greedily sucked the breast dry and bitten it to pieces. In addition, the mastication of food may, at this time and throughout childhood, mean to him the expression of his angry wishes to bite up and devour his parents, a phantasy which must in part be responsible for the dislike of meat, so common among children. Kate (7), when eating cold meat cut into small pieces for her by her mother, thought about chopped-up bodies, dead and cold, and related them in her mind to the Grimm fairy story of the finger which was chopped off the dead body of a rich man by robbers who wanted his ring, and which immediately sprang into the lap of a little girl who was hiding from them. Chloe (2) would eat 'meaties' with relish, but would not touch either chicken or rabbit if the names were mentioned; it seemed that meat was not yet associated with something alive, whereas she had seen and heard stories about chickens and rabbits. The phantasy of the ruthless, cannibalistic child who eats his parents is vividly dramatized in the Russian fairy story of *The Witch Baby*, whose beauty at birth is marred by her black iron teeth, which betray her wicked greed. She grows and grows 'like a seed of corn' filling the whole house, and eventually, having devoured both her parents, sits sucking her thumb and muttering:

'Eaten the father, eaten the mother,
And now to eat the little brother.'

Generally, however, the child is portrayed in fairy stories as innocent and blameless, and it is the parent-figures—the big bad wolf, the ogre and the witch—who threaten to eat the children.

In the case of George (4), whose fears of being attacked emanated from his own strongly aggressive tendencies as discussed in Chapter I, it seemed likely that his very great difficulty in eating arose out of phantasies of the feeding situation as one of mutual attack and destruction. At one point he refused almost everything that was offered to him, but would eat certain things if they were given to him, piece by piece, from his grandmother's plate, so that he himself was not responsible for breaking them up. Sometimes when he had started to eat something whole, like a fishcake, he would reject it after one bite or mouthful, insisting on having it removed from his plate and put out of sight, or if he particularly liked it (as in the case of a jam tart), he would gobble it up very quickly, especially towards the end. Evidently an object which had been bitten or broken into was dangerous to him, and must be got rid of quickly. At times George seemed really frightened of his food: he would watch the mutilated fishcake on his plate almost as if he felt it was alive and would jump up and bite him back.

The episode of the runner beans, described on page 9, provides a key to George's fear of food: it was his own greed that turned it into something persecutory—into snakes, for instance, which would bite and poison him. This 'greed' was constantly being pointed out to him by his mother, whose general relationship with him must have acted as a support to his infantile phantasies of greedily attacking and being attacked back. Whenever she came to visit him, it was a case of which one would 'bite' first, for as soon as they met, either she would start accusing him of some misdeed, or he would begin to grumble, and often they would continue to attack each other verbally throughout the afternoon. Neither of them seemed able or willing to give the other what was wanted: the mother would seek for reassurances that George still loved her, trying in vain to persuade him to kiss her or to sit on her knee, but when he fell down and hurt himself and obviously wanted comfort, she would refuse to pick him up and call him a 'cry-baby'. She would ask him what he wanted for a present, but, as we shall see later, would invariably bring him something of her own choice (generally on the grounds that she disapproved of his aggressive interests), so that he was constantly in the position of being unable to be pleased with something he did not want.

As will be seen in more detail in the next chapter, fears about feeding may relate to phantasies of attacking the mother by means of excretion, the expectation being that the mother whom the child feels he has poisoned with urine and faeces will, of necessity, have only poisoned food to offer him. Tony (8) had an angry scene with his billet-mother one night at bedtime. Later that evening, after he had drunk the cocoa she had brought him and they had said goodnight, he called her back, saying that he had been sick and pointing to some traces of cocoa on the sheet as evidence. He said this had happened because he had drunk poisoned milk that day at school, some boys having prised off the tops of the bottles with pens and squirted ink into it. It seems possible that, in his anger with his billet-mother, Tony (a chronic bedwetter) had wished to attack her with urine in the same way as the boys at school had attacked the milk with ink, but expected that having done so he himself would be poisoned and made sick by the brown (dirty) milk she gave him. Tony also often accused his billet-mother of making him eat beetroot, which he particularly disliked, and which in fact she never gave him, saying that it made 'bad blood' in him, which came out in the form of pus when he had septic spots.

Michael (3) drew bottles of milk which, he said, had been made 'bad and nasty' by his father. Michael was very much tied to his mother, who adored him; she had quarrelled with her husband, a violent, difficult man, and had taken Michael to sleep with her in the bed, while the father slept elsewhere. In Michael's phantasy the father was perhaps jealously revenging himself both on the child for stealing his place with the mother, and on the mother for preferring the child to him; the fact that he poisoned milk might suggest that Michael related the current situation, in which he angered his father by taking his place in the bed, to his early feeding relationship with his mother. This points to the important fact that the early feeding situation can be felt by the child to represent a total love relationship, similar to the relationship between his parents, so that at times he may feel that in having been fed by his mother he successfully displaced his father.

The phantasy of a jealous father who tries to poison both the mother and the child occurred also in the case of Peter, whose feeding difficulties between the ages of three and seven seemed to spring in part from fears of being poisoned by both father and mother. Peter's infantile phantasies of being able to destroy his parents in his anger and hatred must have been terrifyingly confirmed when his father, who was a docker, was killed in an accident at work, and a year later his mother, depressed at the loss of her husband and worried by increasing debts, attempted suicide when alone with Peter in the tenement flat where they lived. She was found lying unconscious on the floor and was taken to hospital, and Peter (3) was subsequently sent to a residential nursery school and did not see her again. He was told by neighbours that she was mad and wicked, and it was hinted that she had tried to kill him as well as herself with white tablets. When he came to the nursery school at the age of four years, Peter could rarely bring himself to speak of her. On one occasion he asked whether she would be likely to be given good food in hospital, and said that he hoped she got enough milk; another time he said he had hated living with her because her flat smelt of corned beef. One night in bed he was asking his teacher how fathers and mothers 'make babies', and she told him that the father put seed into the mother. He then said: 'Yes, I'll tell you how the fathers help the mothers to make babies. They plant some onion seeds in the garden, and they grow onions and give them to the mother to eat, and the onions she eats make the baby inside her, and that's how the father helps.' Immediately afterwards he asked: 'What does it do to the baby if the mother is ill and has tablets when the baby's inside her?' It seems as if Peter was equating onions (white vegetables which he himself disliked) with the white tablets with which it had been suggested his mother had tried to kill both herself and him, and thus was voicing an idea of sadistic sexual intercourse in which the father gave something poisonous to the mother to eat, not only to create a baby but also to kill it.

This phantasy of a father who sought to poison him with bad vegetables was again brought out by Peter when he was discussing his dislike of brussels sprouts. He said that they were dirty, poisonous things which grew in the earth where dead people were buried, and that no amount of washing could make them clean. He then began to speak of his father, saying that he thought he had been killed by Germans when on the way to the bank. Two days before this Peter played at burying dead black horses in a big hole in the garden, calling them 'bad 'uns', and saying that green grass would grow over their grave. It seemed clear that, in Peter's mind, poisonous vegetables that grew in the earth emanated from a dead, bad, dirty father who was buried there. This association between poisonous food and things that grew in the earth was made again by him when he plotted with another boy to plant seeds in the garden of a girl who had annoyed him, which, he said, would grow into poisonous mushrooms and kill her. If the garden can be taken, in each case, to represent the mother's body (cf. 'Mother Earth'), we see here several expressions of the phantasy that the child is poisoned because bad food is put into the mother. In his refusal day after day to eat food given to him by his particular teacher, it seems possible that Peter was expressing fear of a mother who was poisoned and therefore poisonous. He would wander round the room miserably until the meal was finished, and, if urged to sit down and eat, would crouch behind the cupboard whimpering. If later he was offered the same food by someone else, he would quite often eat it without protest, and, providing his teacher was not there, would voluntarily serve himself. When she was there, however, he would always insist that she gave him his food, and would beg her to 'mix it' for him, then refusing to eat it. Thus he seemed compelled continually to bring to life his phantasy of a mother who wanted to poison him, perhaps to prove that he could withstand her attacks.

It is likely that some of the foregoing problems might not have occurred had the infantile phantasies underlying them been modified by a different attitude on the part of the mother towards her baby in the original suckling situation. Through wisdom and gentleness in his mother's handling, a baby can gain confidence which is the basis of ease in personal relationships during the rest of his life. Detailed observation of a number of babies has shown that there are wide differences in response and behaviour while feeding, even in the first few days of life.[1] One baby is eager and confident; another, equally eager, seems over-anxious and unsatisfied. One is sleepy and unable to make an effort; another starts well but soon tires. Although such differences in response are probably partly constitutional and partly due to mechanical factors (shape of nipple, flow of milk, etc.), a baby can be helped considerably by an attitude of patience and confidence on the part of his mother—confidence in his power to take, as much as in hers to give. The mother or nurse who thrusts the nipple or teat into the baby's mouth must surely fail in making a contact with him, and, as already suggested, may give the impression that an attacking breast is being pushed into him, thus intensifying his phantasies. The relationship is most likely to be a satisfactory one if the baby is gently put to the breast and allowed, as far as possible without interference, to take the nipple himself, and if the mother is allowed to have her baby at the breast as soon as they are both well enough after the birth, so that she can begin to get to know him, and he can discover her breast in his own way and in his own time. He then has a chance to find it as a good object, and when later, under the sway of hunger, he has terrifying, greedy impulses, these may be less frightening to both of them, and contact may be more easily made.[2] In establishing a feeding routine, it is best to follow the baby's lead in the first place, and to try to feed him before his need for food has become intense and persecuting; generally, where the baby is fed on demand to begin with, he and his mother are able gradually to settle down to a regular routine which suits both of them.

The relationship between the mother and baby experienced

[1] See Merell P. Middlemore: *The Nursing Couple* (Hamish Hamilton Medical Books).

[2] See D. W. Winnicott: *Getting to Know Your Baby* (The New Era in Home and School, Vol. 26, No. 1).

during the giving and taking of food is expanded and enriched in those moments at the breast when the baby is not actually sucking, but pauses to experiment and play, both with his mouth and hands, and to babble. As he grows older he sucks for increasingly long periods with his eyes open, and may hum or drone in a satisfied way, later becoming able to pause in his feeding to look up at his mother and smile, and to make many varied sounds. There is need for ease and time in the feeding situation to allow for the possibility of interludes in which both mother and baby can enjoy his playfulness, curiosity, and urge to master the intricacies of movement.

From the point of view of an adequate diet, it is generally advisable to start giving the baby some mixed food at a few months, and to have established a full mixed diet by about seven months, but in spite of this it is important not to wean him completely by this time, for he needs the pleasure and satisfaction of sucking for at least nine months and in some cases for longer. Even when he is able to take food satisfactorily from a cup and spoon, he still needs to suck both for enjoyment and comfort, as is shown by the fact that so many children suck their thumbs, and may continue to do so for years at bedtime, or in moments of difficulty. Christopher was weaned completely at the age of five months, and although he always ate well and enjoyed his food, he could not feed at all without at the same time sucking his thumb, until he was about eighteen months old. In general, if new foods and flavours are offered without anxiety and insistence on the mother's part, in very small quantities to begin with, and possibly at the end of a feed when the baby's hunger and need to suck have been satisfied at the breast and he is ready to play, it is likely that he will enjoy them in the same way as he is enjoying other new things in the course of his experiments with his surroundings and his own body.[1] But in whatever way weaning

[1] See Flora Shepherd: *Mixed Feeding for the Breast-fed Baby* (leaflet).

is carried out, it is essential that it should be gradual and gentle, with continued if not extra nursing by the mother. If the baby is weaned too early, or very suddenly and quickly, it may seem like a violent act of retribution; he has far less chance to get used to and accept the situation, and may be overwhelmed with phantasies of punishment and withdrawal of love. In the case of Dinah (see Chapter VII) weaning from the bottle was not begun until eight months, although solids were introduced into her diet gradually from the age of four and a half months. When her first teeth appeared at eight and a half months, she began to prefer to chew the teat rather than to suck it, while at nine and a half months she spontaneously turned from the bottle altogether and only wanted to play at twanging the teat with her finger, developing a great passion for rusks. Thus for this child weaning was by no means only a deprivation, for she herself became ready for new experiences and new modes of gaining satisfaction. The success of weaning does not depend only, however, on how it is managed. Dinah's ability to turn from sucking to biting in such a positive way must have been partly due to the fact that she cut her teeth so late, with the result that her phantasies of attacking by biting at an earlier age were not added to by the apparent biting back of the breast in experiences of pain in her own gums.

In introducing solid foods, it seems wise to follow the child's lead, as in suckling, and to give him opportunity to reject foods which he will possibly return to and accept later. New foods may seem frightening rather than an interesting novelty, and to the child who is forced to eat them the whole process of eating may become a persecution. From this point of view alone, it is helpful to allow the baby scope to handle his food, so that he can investigate anything he feels uncertain about in his own way and at his own time. Towards the end of the first year he generally shows a strong urge to feed himself, and if this is not hampered by the adult's anxiety as to whether he will get enough nourishment, her wish to instil 'table manners' and the use of a spoon from the beginning, or her inability to tolerate mess, this finger-feeding stage is one of great enjoyment, when many experiments are made and the child's individual tastes established. If his urge to master and control his own feeding is thwarted, and he has to be fed neatly and cleanly by his mother with a spoon, and to eat what she ordains without any possibility of choice, an initial period of resistance may soon be followed by resignation and apathy, in some cases resulting in a general attitude of indifference to food as a whole, which can cause the adults much anxiety. Alternatively, willingness to gobble up anything and everything without question is not always to be welcomed and may be a sign of anxiety or immaturity, as in the case of Roddy, who, as he grew more certain of affection, and more of a person in himself, began to be normally selective about his food, establishing certain preferences and dislikes to which he adhered firmly and proudly.

Christopher began to experiment in feeding himself at about six months; his mother did the minimum amount of spoon-feeding, as he always wanted to see exactly what he was eating, and would seize the spoon out of her hand to investigate its contents, sort them out with his fingers, and convey them to his mouth. During the next two years she found it best to allow him to come and go freely at meal-times, and to choose what he would eat from the dishes available, seldom commenting on what he rejected or how much he left. As the result, Christopher had few dislikes, and by the age of two years had learnt to feed himself skilfully. At 2.4 he still liked to play with his food to some extent; for instance, having found that he could float his puffed wheat in his mug of milk, he tried to do the same the next day with his baked beans, while on another occasion he suddenly put his plate of jelly upside down on his head, perhaps in frustration at having spent a considerable time in trying to pick it up with his fingers!

A certain amount of forcing children to eat and inability to permit fads and phases of not eating arises from real concern on the part of the adults for health. This, however, often defeats its own purpose, the adult's anxiety increasing the child's, so that he becomes less able than ever to eat, while if he finds that he can use food fads and periodic refusals to eat to control her, the whole situation may become doubly frightening and develop into a permanent problem, as in the case of Lionel. Temporary faddiness and lack of interest in food are common ways in which children react to periods of special difficulty, and express feelings of anxiety and hostility. Harry, when at the height of his jealousy of Billy, became suddenly fussy and tyrannical over his food. Up till then he had been a hearty eater, with few dislikes; now he began to complain: 'I don't want that', and 'You're giving me too much', but if given a small helping would grumble: 'I don't like a little.' One morning when he asked for 'only a little porridge' his foster-mother gave him one spoonful; having eaten this, he helped himself to all the rest, in spite of protests from his sister Joan who wanted a second helping. The foster-mother's request that Harry should put back some of it resulted in accusations of 'starving' him and a temper tantrum, but to have allowed him to triumph in this situation would probably have left him guilty and anxious. Unconsciously, Harry seemed to be trying to re-capture his foster-mother's interest in him, which he felt had been transferred to Billy, by rousing anxiety in her over his refusals to eat; he was deliberately forcing her to 'starve' him, showing in a dramatic way his feeling that she was depriving him of love; at the same time he was trying to provoke her to anger. On another occasion Harry said that he did not want any tea at all, and so his foster-mother suggested that he should go out and play. When the table was being cleared, Harry reappeared and angrily demanded his tea, but his egg had been eaten by someone else, and there was nothing left but bread and butter. Harry cried bitterly, until his foster-mother said that if he would help her to finish clearing the table, she would then have time to cook him another egg, to which he agreed cheerfully. What seemed to be needed of the foster-mother on these two occasions was some understanding of the child's feelings, together with an ability not only to stand firm, and so demonstrate that she was not being exploited, but also to compromise, thus proving that she was not depriving him of the love he needed so much. If Harry's disturbed feelings had met with anxiety or annoyance on her part, every meal might have developed into a miserable battle, and it is possible that a chronic feeding problem might have been created.

As already suggested, all activities connected with the mouth may be influenced by phantasies arising from the original suckling situation, and may have deeper meanings in terms of loving and preserving, hating and attacking, giving and accepting, depriving and stealing. George would try to blackmail his grandmother with the threat: 'I'll scream your head off!' We talk about 'shattering cries' and 'piercing screams' and this association between screaming and actual bodily attack must relate to very early days when the tiny baby, himself experiencing pain through screaming, felt able to injure and destroy his mother by it. Speech, too, is often felt by both children and adults to be a form of attack: for instance, when Harry was very angry he would shout insults in short, staccato phrases, and seemed to be biting off his words, and when asked what he was doing as he knelt by his bed, imitating his sister who prayed at night, he said: 'I'm saying rude things to the Devil!' The Devil, on the other hand, was stated by Harry to be unable to talk, perhaps because, in Harry's eyes, he would be far too dangerous if able to attack in this way. Harry often complained bitterly that children at school had said 'rude things' about him, and was as grieved as if he had received physical injury. When his foster-mother said it was time for bed and he wished to go on playing, it was her actual statement of the fact which seemed to enrage him most; he said: 'I'd like to put a pin in your mouth so you can't talk!' His speech was very babyish: there were many words which he could produce but generally would not, in spite of encouragement from his foster-mother, so that it seemed partly an attack on her, although clearly, at the same time, an anxious wish to remain a baby. When disturbed by the fact that a father, mother, and baby were staying in the house, he started a persistent, forced cough, often continuing until he made himself sick. At meal-times he would repeatedly cough politely but noisily behind his hand, thus drawing attention to himself; and when sick in bed at night, he seemed to create the maximum mess, making no attempt to use the basin provided. The specific phantasies which lay behind this behaviour were never discovered, but that they related to his foster-mother was shown by the fact that his cough completely cleared up when she went away for two days. He had in the past dirtied himself when angry and jealous (page 46) and it seems that this new, more socialized form of dirtying was also a means of attack (this time by the mouth), as well as of ensuring love and attention, the presence of an unbroken family having re-awakened his feelings of deprivation, anger, and anxiety.

Specific speech difficulties often have a phantasy basis, and may be part of a general personality problem, as in the case of Phyllis, who was a stammerer from the time she started to talk. At six years, she rarely managed to get to the end of a sentence or to produce a whole remark or idea, although she talked continually and made great efforts to express herself clearly. Just as her speech came out in little bits, there was no wholeness about Phyllis or anything she did: she seemed to be purposeless, rarely settling to an occupation or game for more than a short time, finding difficulty in completing any piece of work, and continually being distracted by things which had no relation to what she was doing or to each other, while at nearly all times of the day she had slightly wet knickers, as if even her urine had to come out in drips. She made a great many shallow contacts with people, behaving as if every visitor who came to the house were very important to her, but seemed in general discontented, whining and crying a great deal, as if unable to find what she wanted in anybody or anything. When, with considerable help and encouragement, she managed to finish something like a jigsaw puzzle—in other words, to make a whole out of bits—she seemed both surprised and relieved. When her stammer was at its worst, Phyllis scarcely ever showed aggression openly, but was frequently the victim of other children, and seemed almost deliberately to put herself into this position by arranging situations in which she would be likely to be either attacked or rejected, perhaps thus proving that she herself was not the aggressor. She would join some children who were playing, and then either annoy them or drop out in such a way as to cause discontent, the break-up of the game, and the disintegration of the group; while when she herself organized the game, she would always be running to the adult to complain that another child was spoiling it. Phyllis's whole life had been a series of short episodes: she was illegitimate, sent to an institution, legally adopted, and then sent to another institution when her adoptive mother became mentally ill. Apart from their specific meanings, her stammer and her behaviour could perhaps be seen to express in general a feeling that she herself and her inner world of phantasy figures were in bits, while in actively breaking up sentences, words, streams of urine, and games, she appeared to be constantly living out a phantasy of her own destructiveness.

Thus we see how, in varying ways and at different stages, feelings and phantasies are expressed by the mouth. Later attitudes to eating and drinking, to giving and taking, and to life in general, and ability at every age and stage to make good relationships depend to a very large extent on the child's experiences in the early feeding situation, which, to the tiny baby, is the centre of existence. Respect for his feelings, tenderness to him in the suckling situation, understanding over weaning, and attempts to help him to develop a positive attitude to feeding can make a difference to his development as a person, and his achievement of happiness and independence.

CHAPTER FOUR

Some Meanings of Excretion

As we have seen, the baby's first centre of feeling is his mouth, and as such it remains significant to him throughout life. Nevertheless, even in his earliest days he experiences sensations through other parts of his body, and at a time when urination and defaecation are little more than a chain of reflex actions, there must at least be varying degrees of comfort and discomfort in being wet and dirty. As the baby grows older, however, his anus and urethra become marked sources of excitement. When Dinah was given a soap suppository during a period of constipation at the age of four months, her face became wreathed with smiles, she squirmed with delight, and defaecated with much laughter, so that there was no doubt that the sensations she experienced were highly exciting and pleasurable. Gradually the problems of love and hate, attacking and being attacked, breaking and mending, begin to find expression in excretory processes as well as in mouth activities, urine and faeces acting as vehicles of strong feeling and therefore assuming great significance. Normally, this stage in emotional development reaches its height during the second year, following the period when sucking is all-important.

We know how usual it is for young children to attribute meaning to excretion. Harry (3), although in an environment in which curiosity about all subjects was approved, showed that his attitude to defaecation was far from matter-of-fact, and that he felt it necessary to disguise his interest in it. One night in the bath he talked about washing his feet, indicating his knees; his foster-mother corrected him, and he repeated after her: 'Yes, knees', adding, without conviction: 'These two lumps are knees', but continuing to talk about them as 'feet'. When he was being dried and his legs were about to be rubbed, he suddenly laughed and chanted: 'Hands, knees and poops-a-daisy!' His foster-mother pointed out that it was 'boomps-a-daisy' in the song, but he repeated 'poops-a-daisy' several times with great enjoyment. She then remembered that 'going poops' had been his baby way of talking about defaecation, and so it seemed that his reluctance to accept the word 'knees', which had to be washed because they were 'dirty', and were described as 'lumps', could only be due to their association with stools.

The phantasies which become associated with excretion are, in the first place, not the result of a morality imposed from outside; they spring primarily from the baby's own feelings. When he is happy, contented, and loving, urine and faeces can seem like good things which are welcomed as gifts by his mother. Billy (3) would call out the number and size of his stools with pride: 'One Daddy one and two little ones', or, grudgingly: 'Only one today, not two'; while Christopher (2) would announce with satisfaction: 'Burmeat in my bottom!' in the same way in which he spoke of pennies in his pocket. Dinah, at two years, as will be discussed later, showed clearly that she felt urine to be a good substance which could heal the mother's injured breast, dramatizing this phantasy on several occasions by a game in the bath. At 3.3, when she had a phase of deliberate wetting on the floor, she gave as one reason the fact that her pot was broken and so she could not see her 'wee-wee', adding: 'It goes in the lavatory-water and makes it yellow, and then you wash it away.' Here she seemed to be suggesting that her urine was something too valuable simply to be flushed away down the lavatory without even being looked at. On the basis of the child's own pleasurable physical sensations in urinating and defaecating, the acts of excretion can seem to him like a form of loving physical contact with another person, the experiences being shared; for instance, when Dinah was 1.3, she would cling to her mother with a loving expression when defaecating, and look at her smilingly when urinating. Roddy (4) and Patrick (3) showed from a game they played that defaecating could be an exciting, shared experience, each in turn lifting up his dressing-gown and pretending to 'do ah-ahs' into the other one's mouth, both shouting with hilarious laughter, and demanding the admiration of their teacher. Harry, in the situation over his knees, in which he showed pleasure and excitement, guilt and shame, indicated what a tangled web of phantasy was woven into his attitude to defaecation, and the fact that he associated it with a dance in which adult couples bump their buttocks together suggested that it had the significance of a sexual relationship for him, in which at that moment he was perhaps taking part with his foster-mother, as she washed and dried his knees.

At other times Harry showed by deliberate dirtying and spreading of faeces, with an attitude of defiance towards his foster-mother, that excretion could be used to make a bad relationship. When a child is angry and hating, urine and faeces can be felt to be pushed into the parents, smeared over them or sprayed into them. Albert was an illegitimate child whose mother had to go to work, leaving him to the care of neighbours. When he was three years old, the parents were able to marry, and a year later another baby was born. Albert, although he had been clean for some time, started refusing to use the lavatory or pot, and after sitting for a long time without any result, would go to the bottom of the garden and dirty his trousers. It seems possible that he was not only trying to appeal for the care which he had never had, but also wanted to attack his mother and to injure her for her neglect of him, both now and when he was a baby, although if in defaecating he was hurting his bad, deserting mother, then in going to the end of the garden he was preserving the good mother whom he loved, by doing it as far away from her as possible.

Christopher (2) had a very good relationship with his mother, who treated him with great sympathy and understanding; he was happy and active, and evidently developing well in every respect. His parents had separated, and the father was not seen for some time, after which he began to visit each week-end. He was rather strict and intolerant towards Christopher, who clearly had mixed feelings about him and seemed generally disturbed by his presence, becoming irritable and less easy to manage when he was there. Although usually clean, one of Christopher's regular reactions at the week-end was to wet and dirty his trousers two or three times a day, and instead of appearing distressed and running to his mother crying, which was his usual mode of behaviour on the rare occasions when this happened, he seemed defiant and unconcerned, and did not even let her know about it. It seems likely that, besides being a reaction against his father's severity, Christopher's wetting and dirtying was an expression of resentment that, as an interloper, the father should be there at all, while from his changed attitude to his mother one might deduce that he was attacking her as well, and expressing a jealous fury that his parents should have a relationship together which excluded him. It is not possible to bring out all the motives that lay behind this particualr behaviour, but one can be sure that urine and faeces were being used predominantly as weapons of attack.

The young child expects to be attacked back in the same way as he believes he has attacked his parents or their representatives, and by the same materials; moreover, in his phantasy, urine and faeces are from one point of view not inert and inanimate substances, mechanically produced by the body, but persecutors with a secret and dangerous life of their own. For instance, Harry (4), having dirtied his trousers during rest-time, remarked indignantly and with an aggrieved air: 'It just popped out!'; while Christopher at twenty months would scold and stamp on the puddle he had made on the floor, as if it had arrived of its own volition in order to annoy him; and Dinah (3) would say: 'No, wee-wee, you're not to come out!' and 'The naughty wee-wee came out all by itself!' Actual conscious fear of excrement was experienced by a child who later, as an adult, described an early memory of dirtying her bed when she could have controlled herself, and then sitting on her pillow and looking at a large, dark stool, twisted on itself in the middle of the white sheet. She said that she got the impression that it was alive and dangerous, and felt frightened as well as bitterly ashamed. George (4) would sit on his bed in the daytime and deliberately wet it, and at school would urinate into other children's Wellingtons, and on one occasion played a game in which he held a leather strap between his legs and went around pretending to shoot people, saying: 'Pish-sh-sh-sh!' It was perhaps the strength of the aggressive feelings underlying his wetting activities which made him feel that water was dangerous, for he would not go near the river, nor get into a bath which he thought was too deep, in case he was drowned. In the case of Christopher (2), the name 'burmeat' (bird's meat) was given to faeces, to meat (which he always ate with great avidity), and to a duck's beak on his aunt's mantelpiece towards which he showed much fear. Thus is seems likely that to him faeces were from one point of view good to eat, but from another dangerous and frightening.

One can well imagine that the burning, stinging, and cutting sensations caused by urine can be felt to be actively brought about by a hostile person, and that when the child's faeces give him pain (as when he is constipated) they may seem like bad people or parts of them attacking him from inside in retaliation for his attacks on them. From this point of view they need to be got rid of, and if retained may cause anxiety. Some eight- to nine-year-old children who had had teaching at school on the subject of elimination, in discussing this afterwards repeatedly stressed the point that faeces were composed of bad, poisonous, dead food which could not safely be left in the body. At all ages constipation may lead to many anxieties about being attacked from within, and having something bad inside which 'poisons the system'. It is striking how in any hospital ward, worry about constipation is almost universal amongst convalescent adult patients, even ' though they are reassured that it is to be expected under certain circumstances, and frequently recovery and the ability to pass a motion are equated in a patient's mind, immense relief being expressed when regular habits are re-established.

On the other hand, as was suggested in the case of Albert, a child can feel forced to withhold his faeces, both because they are dangerous things which must not be allowed into the open, and because the act of defaecating itself can be felt to be a form of attack. At the same time, one can see withholding as an aggressive act, often combined with an attitude of obstinacy in general. In other cases it can be the child's effort to keep good things inside him, with the fear of being robbed by his mother when she demands that he give up his faeces to order: he may feel that she is trying to take away essential parts of him or precious objects in retaliation for his wish to rob her and his father. To Dinah faeces were at one time clearly babies. Some weeks after her brother was born (when she was 3.4) she insisted that *her* baby was going to come out of her 'back pilly' (anus) and that she could feel it at night, explaining: 'The baby must come out like that because it slides.' When her mother asked: 'But how would you know if it was a baby or a big job?' she replied: 'It makes a different noise, a clapping noise.' On another occasion she said: 'It must hurt to have a baby.'

Mother: 'Who told you that?'

Dinah: 'I told myself.'

Mother: 'Why does it hurt?'

Dinah: 'It's too big and stiff and it blocks up the wee-wee.'

On being told by her mother that babies did not come out of the anus but out of another special hole, Dinah compromised by saying of her doll: 'Well anyway, Libberbel came out of my back pilly because she's an unusual baby!'

Peter, whose feeding problems were described in Chapter III, was greatly preoccupied with matters of excretion. He frequently wet his bed, having wrapped his sheet and on one occasion his bath-towel round him like a nappy. When discussing what it could be that caused his bed-wetting, he said that he thought it was because he was having 'exciting fun in the night' and also that he had been thinking of 'nasty things like witches and sword-fencing'. He would spend long periods sitting on the lavatory, would smear the wall with faeces, and on occasions would wipe himself on the lavatory cloth or on the bath mat or other children's flannels which he had collected from the bathroom next door, and which, when soiled, he would hide away in a hole in the wall above the lavatory cistern, while once he was found to have placed a piece of used toilet paper on his dressing table. In looking for further light on Peter's problems, one cannot avoid the link between his concern with urine and faeces, and his concern with the food he was going to eat. It will be remembered that, at the age of four years, he said his dislike of brussels sprouts was due to the fact that they could not be washed clean because they grew in the dirty brown earth, apparently associating them with dead (bad) people who were buried there—in particular, his own father. A year later, he openly identified food he disliked with dogs' and cows' 'muck', and it was once reported that he

78

and another child had discussed the comparative size and merits of their potatoes (cooked in their skins) in terms of penises, as with enjoyment they chopped them up. Thus it is clear that in Peter's mind there was an association between unpleasant food, the body of his dead father, and faeces. Moreover the conversation between Peter and his teacher described on page 61 showed that he believed babies to be both created and killed by the eating of onions, and in view of the fact that these are strong-smelling vegetables which grow in the ground, they, too, clearly represented faeces. Thus faeces were to him not only a form of poison but at the same time highly exciting substances, with which one could have a sexual relationship. His assumption of a nappy before he wet his bed showed clearly his identification with a baby, but his 'exciting fun in the night' and his thoughts about 'nasty things like witches and sword-fencing' might suggest that in urinating he was also identifying with the parents in a cruel intercourse situation, the sword-fencer possibly representing the father who, with cutting urine, penetrates the bad (sexual) witch-mother.

Tony, already referred to, was at eight years another confirmed bed-wetter. He said that he liked the feeling of being warm and wet, and on one occasion suggested that there was something magic about urinating. He seemed to be unashamed about his bed-wetting, saying that he could stop it if he wished to, and on two occasions did in fact stop—once for ten days when someone promised him a parcel if he were dry, and another time for a week, when given a chart on which he coloured squares representing dry nights. Although various people tried to 'cure' Tony in ways of this kind, he seemed basically impervious to superficial encouragement and help, and eventually it became clear that he could give up bed-wetting only if offered a satisfying substitute, since becoming dry was not something desirable to him in itself. A bargain was made between Tony and his billet-mother in which every evening following a dry night Tony was to have late supper with an older child (in addition to his usual high tea). The bed-wetting eventually ceased, although for a time he continued to wet his bed every Thursday, explaining that he did not want to *have* to stay up to supper the following night, as on Friday it was always fish, which he disliked. It is evident that this was only a symptomatic cure; it is, however, interesting to note the particular form of gratification which could be accepted by Tony as a substitute, in that it may perhaps suggest something of the meaning of bed-wetting to him. It seems possible that supper, an adult occasion which takes place at night and from which children are generally excluded, could have symbolized for him parental night-time activities from which he was debarred; as we shall see later in a play directed by Tony, sexual intercourse seemed to be represented by him as a feast by candlelight. Thus bed-wetting, with its 'magic' quality, may have been Tony's attempt to obtain pleasure similar to that of his parents, while in view of the fact that his general pattern of behaviour was to interfere ruthlessly with other people's pleasures, it seems possible that he was also 'swamping' their activities.

Diana (10) also gave some indication of the underlying meaning of her long-standing, inexplicable bed-wetting. She was an intelligent girl, who had a strong conscious wish to find the reason for it and to cure herself. One day she remarked that her dry nights always seemed to go in twos, and that she never managed to 'make it three'. When asked what 'two' made her think of, she immediately said: 'Mummy and Daddy'; this led to memories of sleeping in her parents' room, her cot always being next to her mother, because, she said, her father liked to smoke in bed. This suggests that Diana's bed-wetting might have been connected with early phantasies of wanting to make a third with her father and mother, that is, to take part in their intercourse. But because she never managed it, she felt she could only have two consecutive dry nights, although in reality she sometimes had much longer dry periods. The fact that this problem should have been repeatedly acted out in the process of bed-wetting suggests not only that it was still active, but also that her original reaction to her feelings of jealousy was to attack her parents by wetting, perhaps thus interrupting them by diverting the mother's attention from the father to her. Also, Diana's memory of her father smoking in bed as something from which the baby was kept away could have been unconsciously related to experiences of seeing her parents in intercourse, and could suggest confusion of the male role with a burning activity, which might lead one to think that in wetting her bed she was not only trying to separate them but also identifying herself with each of them in their relationship together by actively producing burning urine, which in its turn burnt her. She implied that if she could 'make it three' she would be able to give up bed-wetting altogether, but the fact that she was convinced that this was impossible suggests that there was a strong element of guilt working against her efforts to create a triangular relationship, so that wetting at the same time gratified the wish and appeased the guilt.

Like bed-wetting, smearing of faeces may be a child's way of expressing feelings in concrete, pre-verbal terms. Where it suddenly appears as a sympton, it may point to the fact that some particular current anxiety has reawakened an early conflict. Dorothy (9), the only child of devoted parents, shocked her convent boarding-school by smearing the lavatory walls, especially as she was a particularly well brought-up, fastidious, and self-respecting child, who was rather shy and reserved. It proved on investigation that, though her parents never quarrelled and gave the impression of being united, her father had become infatuated with a casual acquaintance and her mother was basically unhappy about it; moreover, although they visited Dorothy together every week-end, they had temporarily closed the home on the grounds that they were both working. Dorothy seemed to be making a desperate attempt to shock her parents into realizing her feelings; in a way, she was openly blazing them on the wall, but, perhaps because she unconsciously felt that whatever was wrong with her parents' relationship, it must be a dirty secret since it could not be spoken about, she chose a dirty, secret way of expressing them. She may also have been labelling her parents as dirty people by smearing *them*, and showing the world that their apparently normal relationship, which looked as unspoiled as the clean wall, was really only whitewashed. Dorothy's specific phantasies never came to light, but as the parents gained more understanding of the situation and made a home again, their relationship becoming a truly and not just an apparently good one, her smearing ceased, and there seemed no doubt that it had been related to her phantasies about the whole situation.

In the practical handling of such problems as smearing, bed-wetting, and dirtying prolonged beyond early childhood, it seems generally of most help actively to encourage and support the child's conscious wish to be 'cured', which is not just a wish to gain adult approval, but also a need to feel himself capable of becoming grown-up and controlled. At the same time one may realize, accept, and where possible make alternative provision for the unconscious wish to remain a baby, or to obtain gratification in these infantile ways. The smearing of a boy in a Children's Home ceased when he was given an outside lavatory to himself, labelled 'G. Johnson. Private.' It was suggested that he should decorate the walls and door with paintings, which he did in a lavish manner, and he himself undertook the task of keeping it clean, often choosing to spend Sunday mornings giving it 'a good scrub-out'. Perhaps this opportunity to smear paint gave him the means of expressing his phantasies in a socialized way, while his interest in the cleanliness of his lavatory still allowed for concern with dirt. In the case of Tony, we have seen how late supper was accepted as a substitute for bed-wetting; he would eat it with much satisfaction, and often cooked it for himself with evident pleasure in his achievement. Another chronic bed-wetter, Myra (10), took great pride in a new hot-water bottle, which had been given to her after a dry period. But Terence (7), who was promised a bicycle if he stopped wetting the bed, was found to be getting up almost every hour throughout the night, in order to ensure that he was dry. It seemed that this reward was both too exciting and too far-removed from his bed-wetting, and that it savoured too much of bribery. It also seemed to be putting too much strain on the child, first in demanding a whole series of dry nights before he got his one big reward, and secondly in laying him open to the guilt of lapsing again, in which case the reward would have been given to him on false pretences and his parents cheated. What appears to be needed is some form of comfort, which is no great loss to the child if he fails to achieve it, especially if he still has a chance to gain it on other nights.

The value of encouragement and praise was shown in the case of Peter at the residential nursery school. He showed much pride in achieving a dry bed, springing up and embracing his teacher on being called in the mornings, shouting: 'Another one!' This contrasted strongly with his attitude to bed-wetting of a few months earlier, when he was in conflict with an assistant who did not easily tolerate it, and who, he seemed to feel, did not help him over it as much as she helped another child. He would say defiantly last thing at night: 'Well, *I'm* going to have a wet bed as usual!' although his underlying wish to be cured and the extent to which he was prepared to go to try to help himself was shown at one point by his insistence on drinking several glasses of milk (which he disliked) before going to bed, because he had heard from someone that bed-wetting was provoked by not drinking enough.

Although in effecting such symptomatic cures through environmental help the child's main problem may remain untouched, and the result may be the production of another symptom instead, there is at least the overcoming of something which is essentially a major social handicap. Also in the case of every successful 'cure' there is likely to be some degree of satisfaction and reassurance to the child, however strong were the underlying urges to continue wetting and dirtying, and resistances to becoming clean.

In general, an easy-going, casual attitude towards the whole matter of excretion seems to be of most help. A rigid, over-anxious demand for adherence to routine may successfully lead to the early establishment of clean and regular habits, and may seem to fulfil the child's physical needs, but this is often at the expense of his personality as a whole, quite apart from sometimes leading to relapses at a later age. In persuading him that it is essential always to defaecate at a particular time, and in insisting that he sit on the pot or lavatory until he has done so, we are likely to confirm his phantasies about the bad things inside him which must be got rid of, and in investing the whole process of excretion with importance and showing anxiety ourselves, we suggest that there really is a basis for his fears. We may build up in him an attitude to life in general that it is vital for everything always to be under control, and for things to happen only at a set time and in a particular way, so that he becomes enslaved to routine and can never leave anything to chance, lest his destructive impulses should get the upper hand and cause unutterable damage. His fear of not doing the right thing in the right place and at the right time may lead, in adult life, to indecisiveness and inability to take action. Moreover, if we insistently demand his faeces, we are likely to confirm for him his phantasies of greedy, retributive parents, with the result that he may become mean and miserly. Also, if we lay undue emphasis on the whole matter of excretion, we may strengthen his phantasies about the exciting sexual aspect of it to such an extent that his emotional development is arrested at this stage.

Where the adults are not worried about excretory functions, children tend to establish their own routines without anxiety, although it is important to realize that toilet-training, carried out in a mild and undemanding way and at the right moment, can be of great positive value to a child. It does not consist merely in the deprivation of infantile pleasures at the demand of social standards, but is of reassurance to him, showing him that he can be controlled and grown-up. Chloe at the age of two and a half years still wore nappies at night, and slept in a cot from which she could not get out on her own. Every evening she would scream for her mother, saying she wanted to use her pot, but would not urinate when put on it, and this situation would be repeated over and over again, sometimes for hours on end, until Chloe eventually fell asleep exhausted. If she later woke and found herself wet, she would sob bitterly. In the daytime she would always refuse to defaecate into her pot, however long she was left on it, and would regularly dirty her nappy at rest time, and then cry until she was picked up and changed. The mother would show irritation and disgust or a resigned indifference if Chloe were wet or dirty, but she never really helped her to be clean, as although she would sit her on the pot at regular intervals, she usually did so in a rough, business-like way, and never gave her the opportunity to be independent in the matter. She did not care enough about her to recognize her underlying need to become controlled and self-reliant, and so Chloe's babyish dependence on her was fostered and her infantile gratification from wetting and dirtying prolonged. The fact that this situation was far from satisfying to Chloe herself was shown by her evident distress at wetting her bed night after night, and dirtying her pram day after day.

A sharp contrast in the mother's general attitude, and specifically in her handling of toilet-training, is provided by the case of Christopher. As already implied, Christopher's relationship with his mother was mutually easy and happy-go-lucky, with much acceptance on either side. By the age of 1.4 he had given up nappies, although he was not by any means always clean and dry, and just before he was 2.0 he was moved out of his cot into a low bed. Although he still wet his bed from time to time, if he woke in the night he would sometimes get out of bed, pick up his pot, take it over to his mother, and wake her up to hold it for him. Once or twice when she was not in the room he managed to use it by himself, and on one occasion, when 2.4, was found sleepily making his way to the lavatory at midnight. As already described, apart from the week-ends when his father was there, Christopher showed some distress on the rare occasions when he dirtied himself, although his attitude to a certain amount of wetting was quite matter-of-fact. In general he appeared unanxious, but showed positive goodwill towards becoming clean and a wish to take the matter into his own hands. This attitude of Christopher's was obviously influenced by the mother's corresponding lack of anxiety; if he showed any distress, she would always reassure him, but at other times she would protest from the practical point of view, saying, with no air of grievance: 'Oh, Chrissie, you are a wretched boy!—that's the third pair of trousers this afternoon!'

Sometimes, in the case of quite young children, wetting and dirtying, far from being calmly taken for granted, are a source of great anxiety, in spite of a helpful and tolerant attitude on the part of the adults. Billy (3), at a time when he was showing guilt about wetting his bed, would be tense and miserable when saying goodnight to his foster-mother, calling her back over and over again with much crying. Often, having been left apparently reassured, he would later begin to cry and call her back again.

One night he was most reluctant to let her go and repeatedly wanted her to kiss his 'bad' nose, and then to kiss hers. Soon after she left, he called her back, screaming that he had bitten his tongue. She comforted him and he was soon talking cheerfully and wanting to start kissing noses again. He asked for his handkerchief out of the pocket of his dungarees to dry his tears, which his foster-mother gave him, but as soon as she started to go he called her once more, first to put it back in his pocket, and then to give it to him again. She put it under his pillow, but he immediately began screaming for it to go into his pocket. His foster-mother transferred it again and said goodnight, but he was soon calling for her to come back once more, this time to fasten up all the buttons of his dressing-gown, which was hanging on the door. It seemed as if Billy needed things to be made safe, and that all his demands were attempts to control the situation, and to keep his foster-mother there to protect him against himself. As no ordinary reassurances seemed to help, his foster-mother felt she should show him that she understood something of the meaning of the situation, and suggested that he needed his handkerchief to dry his wet eyes because they were like a wet bed, and that he was frightened of being wet; it was his 'wee-wee' that he felt was 'bad', not his nose, she said, and so he wanted her to make it better by kissing it. Billy then seemed less anxious, said goodnight cheerfully, went to sleep without recalling her, and did not wet his bed.

Although the specific phantasies underlying Billy's bed-wetting were not apparent, it is clear that he was reassured when his foster-mother showed him that she recognized his anxiety about it. In general, it is helpful to realize that all acts of excretion in early childhood have their phantasy meanings, and are never simply humdrum matters of nursery routine. In expressing love and hate, guilt and concern, they are important to the child, and the adults' acceptance of this contributes to his personality development.

CHAPTER FIVE

Genital Feelings and Phantasies

THE fact that from an early age genital sensations are experienced has now been established, and is constantly being confirmed by people caring for babies and young children. Christopher, during his second year, would clutch his penis when excited or when being cuddled, and at two years, in a very happy mood, would sometimes exclaim laughingly: 'Oh, my wee-wee!' Dinah (1.11) touched her genitals as she lay on the bed one day, and shouted with delighted laughter, saying: 'Bottom!' and some weeks later, while in the bath, she said: 'I like my bottom; I want my bottom; Mummy, let I play with my bottom.' Young children sometimes show that they are interested in and want to touch, display, and inspect their own and other children's genitals. In the history of Dinah, given in Chapter VII, there are many instances of frank question and discussion expressing great interest in and concern over these matters, and an unashamed investigation of herself leading to such comments as: 'Little boys have got tailies there, but I haven't. What have I got?' 'That's a little taily, and the wee-wee lives in there'; and 'Jimmy has a tiny weeny taily, and when he grows up he will have a huge enormous taily like his daddy Peter and my daddy Ben, and then everyone will have two daddies.' In a free and unprejudiced environment, young children will often express such interest in genital organs, but the fact that it is not simply a conscious, intellectual, and scientific one, but is coloured by emotion and is the centre of much unconscious phantasy, is shown by the way in which it is sometimes masked and expressed indirectly, with a high degree of excitement, in spite of the absence of concern or disapproval on the part of the adults. Harry (4) had a balloon which was partly deflated; he commented over and over again on its 'nose' with loud, exaggerated laughter, twisted and pressed it, and thrust it at people aggressively, yet with embarrassment. There was an air of tension until his foster-mother said: 'Don't you mean its wee-wee?'—at which Harry, in a milder way and with evident relief, said: 'Yes, look—I'm pushing it in. I push *my* wee-wee in and out sometimes.''

It seemed as if Harry gained relief from finding that his foster-mother was not shocked, as he himself seemed to be, by the activities of the balloon and their implications in terms of his own penis, that is, by his masturbation (which will be discussed later), and by the thrusting activity of the penis, of which he appeared to have some unconscious awareness. Work in psycho-analysis has pointed to the fact that children have an innate unconscious knowledge of their genital function, and that sexual drive begins early in life. There seems to be little evidence of this in the overt behaviour of babies, although one might associate it with the well-known fact that boys, from infancy, show absorbed interest in things that move along, such as engines, aeroplanes, and cars. Christopher, during his first year, before he could be said to have reached the stage of imitative and imaginative 'motor' play, repeatedly made bumping and thrusting movements with any object that came to hand, accompanied by effortful, grunting noises. He would also make the same droning noise when pushing along a spoon or brick as he made when urinating, even in his sleep. Roddy, at four years, showed clearly an awareness of genital function when one day in the garden he ran up to his nursery school teacher, sat astride her, put a ball between his legs, and pushed it hard against her, laughing triumphantly and saying in a loud, gruff voice: 'I'm Mr. Jones!'—the gardener who was much admired by Roddy. Harry, at the same age, went early one morning to see his foster-mother who was still in bed, and got in beside her underneath the eiderdown. She said: 'Your knee's sticking into my stomach; don't keep bumping me, it hurts'—at which Harry replied: 'I'm bumping your bottom with my nose.' As will be seen more fully from later material, Harry often equated nose and penis.

In the play activities of little girls, too, one recognises certain feminine traits and interests which might suggest unconscious knowledge of sexual function: apart from concern with dolls and with games of 'mothers and fathers', there is often pleasure in accumulating and arranging possessions, in arraying a dressing-table or mantelpiece with small things, in owning little boxes to keep things in, and having the right sort of pencil-case or paint-box. One of the favourite games of Dinah at 2.5 was to make 'secrets' in boxes and to build brick houses with ceilings, completely enclosing a little dog or 'little Mr. Brick', then saying: 'You can't see him.' There are also such activities as making books of stories and poems, and keeping diaries or notebooks containing friends' addresses and birthdays or pressed flowers. The commonness of all these interests might suggest that the girl is concerned with the question of having a place in which to receive and conserve special things—that is, that unconsciously she has some concept of herself as a person whose function is to cherish and care for something valuable inside her.

Roddy with his ball and Harry in his foster-mother's bed both showed that they recognized and were interested in genital function in terms of a relationship between two people. In both cases there had probably been opportunities of witnessing parental intercourse, but this knowledge has been expressed so often and so clearly in the phantasies and play of children who are known to have had no such experiences, that it is now believed to be innate.

In children's phantasies, sexuality is not always seen in genital terms; for instance, as we have seen in the case of Harry, defaecation had at times the significance of a relationship, while Peter imagined that the father gave onions (representing faeces) to the mother to eat in order to create a baby. A child's conception of intercourse is inevitably based on his own physical experiences and coloured by his own sensations, feelings, and wishes: he may believe that the parents are feeding from each other, sucking fluid out of or spitting or excreting into each other. Such activities may seem to him highly enviable, and he may long to take part in the relationship himself—to make a third, as in the case of Diana (see p. 80)—or to take the place of father or mother and so have the other parent to himself. Many parents have found it difficult to deal with the problem of the child who bursts into their bedroom at night, often in a suspicious or aggrieved way, and demands to be taken into their bed. The child in this situation feels left out, deserted and attacked, as if the parents were combined against him. In his anger and jealousy, he has phantasies of successfully alienating them, feeling that he is able to turn the relationship into one of dangerous warfare in which the parents attack each other in ways in which he himself is used to attacking in phantasy—by biting and swallowing up, drowning, poisoning, suffocating, and burning.

At the same time as feeling excluded from the situation, the child omnipotently feels that he takes part in it, and his phantasy is brought to life by the excitement he gains through his own masturbation, which, like bed-wetting, can have the meaning of joining in and at the same time interfering with the parental relationship. The child's physical pleasure in masturbating embodies phantasies both of the fulfilment of sexual impulses towards the parents, and of the satisfaction of his aggressive wishes to force his way into the relationship. It is such phantasies of attack and destruction that are the basic causes of guilt about masturbation, persisting in spite of uncritical acceptance and reassurance on the part of the adults.

Harry, during a period of several months, was known to be masturbating more than usual, both at night-time and during the day, and the fact that he was deeply concerned with the feelings and phantasies which related to it was evident in his bedtime conversations with his foster-mother. For instance, one night she had said goodnight to him, and some time later stopped and went in to speak to Billy, who slept in the next room. Harry heard her and began to cry, complaining that his finger was hurting. He continued to whimper without relief from her reassurances, until she asked whether his finger had been bad, at which he immediately stopped crying and said: 'It's only been in the bed. I was lying on it. It was underneath me.' His foster-mother suggested that he might be angry with his finger for playing with his penis, and was therefore hurting it to punish it. Harry first denied this, saying that he could not help his finger hurting, and then said, with tears: 'I don't like my finger playing with my wee-wee; it makes me sick in my mouth.'

Another night he begged, in tears, for his bedroom light to be left on. His foster-mother asked him what he did not like about the dark.

Harry: 'It makes me sick.'

Foster-mother: 'What do you see?'

Harry: 'I saw my dressing-gown; it was shaking up and down.'

Foster-mother: 'What made it?'

Harry: 'The wind; it came through the window.'

Foster-mother: 'What did it look like?'

Harry: 'Sort of red things on it. I don't like it coming to my eyes; it made me jump.' (*Then, anxiously watching his foster-mother's face:*) 'I shall bite off all my nails!'—at which he angrily pretended to do so, as if trying to injure himself. In view of the fact that here again it was Harry's fingers which needed to be punished (bitten off), one might feel that what frightened and distressed him when left alone in the dark was his own masturbation, making him jump and feel sick, and shaking him up and down like a dressing-gown in the wind.

On another evening the following conversation took place:

Harry: 'I look like crying.'

Foster-mother: 'Why?'

Harry: 'My eyes are watering because of my cold.'

Foster-mother: 'Where is your cold?'

Harry: 'In my tummy' (*indicating his penis, and apparently masturbating*).

Foster-mother: 'I shouldn't do that to yourself if I were you.'

Harry (*indignantly*): 'I'm not *picking*!'

Foster-mother: 'Do you sometimes pick?'

Harry: 'Yes, I pick my wee-wee.'

Foster-mother: 'Why?'

Harry: 'Because it sticks on my leg.' (*Laughing:*) 'Crocodiles don't eat sticks, I mean dicks!' (*this repeated with much laughter*).

Foster-mother: 'Do you mean crocodiles don't eat wee-wees?'

Harry: 'Yes.'

It seems likely that here Harry was thinking of castration and trying to deny his anxiety by laughing, probably partly in defence against his foster-mother's attitude of mild reproof towards his masturbation.

On another occasion, when being dried after his bath, Harry remarked: 'Once I cried when I wet my bed.' On being asked why, he replied: 'Because a dog got in it and bit off my nose.' Harry's associations here between crying, bed-wetting, and losing his nose, and in the earlier conversation between crying, having a cold (a running nose), masturbation, and losing his penis, suggest that bed-wetting and masturbation were equated in his mind as activities punishable by castration. As we shall see later, the crocodile often stood in Harry's dreams for his father, and so it would seem that it was his father he feared would castrate him. This was perhaps also suggested by the fact that he had many dreams in which his father ruthlessly interfered with his activities and attacked him, as for instance: 'I was winding a crane, and it wouldn't go up, only down, and it was elefo hard, and then my Daddy came with a sports car and crashed into it and the crane went 'snap!' '

Harry's feelings towards his father were violent and mixed: at times he boasted of his father's great strength, which he saw as employed in assault and destruction, sometimes in his defence, but more often in attack on him. He felt persecuted by him in two particular ways. In the first place, he believed that his father, who was a car dealer and drove about in a sports car, had promised to bring him a toy one, but this never materialized and was a constant source of grievance, causing crying and rather babyish behaviour. In the second place, Harry had continually to remind himself of the painful fact that his father seldom visited him, that he often did not come when he had said he would, and that he generally stayed only for a very short time when he did come. Certain remarks of Harry's showed that, in his mind, his father's neglect of him was linked with the fact that he was a boy. Walking along the road one day, he said: 'When I'm grown-up and change into a girl, I shall have all my teeth out.' When his foster-mother asked him why he wanted to change into a girl, he replied: 'Because my Daddy doesn't come and see me any more.' Here he seemed to be saying that only if he became a girl by having his teeth out (that is, by being castrated) would his father love and visit him. On another occasion he said: 'When I'm grown-up and a farmer, I'll be my father's daughter.' The longing for him to give him a sports car—something with which he could do good, constructive, masculine things—might suggest that he wanted to be reassured that his father would allow him to be a boy; as things were, however, he was left with the feeling that he hated him for his masculinity. That Harry believed that his father's negative attitude sprang from jealousy of him as rival and interloper in the parental relationship was suggested by many of his dreams and phantasies, as will be described later.

Harry's feelings about his mother were not expressed directly, for he spoke of her seldom, and generally only with reluctance; this probably being partly due to his having been told repeatedly by his father: 'You haven't got a Mummy now; she wasn't any use to you, and you don't need to think about her any more.' Feelings about her and phantasies about his relationship with her were, however, vividly expressed towards his foster-mother. He showed his wish to have a close and intimate contact with her, to possess and control her, and his demands for kisses and cuddling quickly changed to angry hitting when she had to turn her attention to something or someone else. He would often become highly excited when she said goodnight to him, making half-affectionate, half-aggressive attacks on her and laughing delightedly, but clinging tearfully when it was time for her to leave.

Harry's wish to have her exclusively to himself and his jealous fear of her relationships with other people were shown clearly in his attitude to her friends and visitors, before whom he would behave in an aggressive way, anxiously and discontentedly making many more demands on her than usual, and showing much resentment at the least frustration or deprivation imposed on him by the situation. When Don, her nephew, came to stay on his leaves from the Army, Harry would try to enlist his support and turn him against her. For instance, on one occasion when she was displeased with him and would not allow him to play in her room that evening, Harry got permission from Don to go to his room instead. There he made a great deal of mess with a bottle of ink, spilling it over the bed and armchair. His attitude to the whole situation was one of both guilt and anger: it seemed likely that he felt guilty at having managed to get from Don the good thing his foster-mother had refused him, implying that he had successfully won him over to his side and created disagreement between them, while his anger was perhaps with Don for being so easily won over and exploited. In spilling the ink, Harry was perhaps depicting the mess he felt he had made of their relationship; or he may have been showing that he felt he had 'blackened' Don by turning him against the foster-mother. On the other hand, one of Harry's happiest experiences was the occasion when the two of them took him to the cinema. The excitement of the film, which concerned the abandoning of a burning, sinking ship and the eventual rescuing of it, and the satisfaction of sitting between them in the dark made a deep impression on Harry, and he was still recalling the details, with intense pleasure, months later. Perhaps it signified to him having loving parents, friendly both to each other and to him, and being admitted and even welcomed to the centre of their relationship.

Harry's concern with the parental relationship and with the part he felt he himself played in it was shown in a number of dreams and stories which he related to his foster-mother during the year in which his masturbation seemed to reach its height—between the ages of 4.0 and 5.0. In some of these phantasies the figures were spontaneously identified by Harry as his father, mother, and himself, while feelings expressed in daily situations towards his father and foster-mother were dramatized in relation to these phantasy figures. There was generally tension and excitement in the narration of them, with an acute need to tell particular dreams, followed by decrease in anxiety when they were accepted with understanding. Harry's phantasies were normal for his age and stage of development; at the same time, they were probably intensified by the facts of his home background, and by experiences gained in sharing his parent's bedroom, which, in view of what was known about his home, seemed likely to have happened up to the age of three years.

The following phantasy was related by Harry in the course of bedtime conversation:

Harry: 'My mummy's dead.'

(*Harry's foster-mother queried this, saying that she thought his mother was not dead, but had gone away.*)

Harry: 'No she's dead. She's killed. I saw her killed. The bad 'un came to my daddy's house and killed her.'

Foster-mother: 'What was he like?'

Harry: 'Like—like the ceiling' (*pointing to a long shadow*). 'He had a gun like that, and held it like this and went click-click, and I saw my mummy fall down killed.'

Foster-mother: 'And then what happened?'

Harry (laughing): 'I said: "What you doing, killing my mummy?" And he said: "I'll shoot you too!" And I ran upstairs, and the policeman came to my daddy's house and said: "What you doing, killing that mummy?" And he killed him himself. And I was the policeman, *and* I was the bad 'un, and then I turned into Harry. It was elefo funny! I was nearly killed too!'

On another occasion he announced: 'I'm going to have a nice dream.'

Foster-mother: 'What about?'

Harry (after a long pause): 'Well, there were some fishes.'

Foster-mother: 'Yes?'

Harry: 'No—there were some cats, and the cat ate the fish, and the fish was dead, and then it came alive, and the cat ran after it and ate it.' (*Inspecting his foster-mother's ears*): 'You've got a hole in it!'

Foster-mother: 'Don't you remember when I used to wear ear-rings? They went through those holes, and that's how they stayed on.'

Harry: 'You looked like a lady when you had ear-rings.' (*Looking round the room*): 'Do—er—cupboards make holes?'

Foster-mother: 'Do you mean do people make holes in cupboards? Perhaps you are wondering how people make holes in ears. They make them with a needle. It doesn't hurt much, and then the ear-rings can fit in.'

Harry: 'Ugh! If I was a rabbit and was shot in the bottom!'

Foster-mother: 'What would happen?'

Harry: 'My daddy would make me alive again.'

In one particular series of phantasies, related almost daily for some weeks, the central figures were crocodile, bulldog, and horse. Once or twice the crocodile was expressly indentified by Harry as his father; it seems likely that the idea came from a book in the *Little Black Sambo* series which was a great favourite with Harry and had to be read aloud to him over and over again. In this story the crocodile pushes its head into a little girl's jar and breaks it, causing her to get into trouble with the cross old woman who is her guardian; the guardian is then swallowed by the crocodile, lights a fire inside him, and blows them both up into bits. Bulldogs were very much on Harry's mind, for one called Maggie sometimes broke into the school playground and terrified him with her incalculable and apparently fierce behaviour. Horses appeared in several phantasies, and generally behaved in a tiresome, interfering way; for instance, in one dream a horse who was being thrown up into the air by a crocodile was identified by Harry as Billy, the little boy whose entry into his foster-family Harry had so much resented. The following are two examples in this series, both related on the same day:

'A crocodile was chasing a bulldog, and a horse was chasing the crocodile. The crocodile got into a house and sat down, and he was angry with the horse for chasing him.'

'We had a lovely time at the museum. We saw elephants and fishes and snakes and crocodiles and birds and bulldogs. And I saw a car going so fast it crashed into a bulldog, and a crocodile was hiding behind a tree, and the crocodile opened its mouth and bust off his doors, and it bust off his driver's handle, and I was scared. But the driver didn't want a handle—he wanted to work it without. He didn't want one that went this way' (indicating forwards), 'but one that went backwards instead. And we saw fishes—one wocking great fish. And I was the driver of the car.'

Throughout all these phantasies ran the idea of a destructive relationship: the mother was killed by a 'bad 'un' with a gun, the cat repeatedly swallowed and killed the fish, women's ears were pierced, rabbits were shot in the bottom, the crocodile chased the bulldog, and the car crashed into her. There were generally three participants in the drama, and in two instances Harry expressly identified himself with the character who pursued and damaged another character and was violently attacked by the third: that is, he was the interfering child who aggressively tried to achieve a relationship with the mother, and was punished by the jealous and angry father, presumably with castration—his driver's handle was 'bust off'. On the other hand, at the same time as being the 'bad 'un' who killed the mother (a phantasy which perhaps seemed confirmed for him by her actual disappearance) he was also the policeman who tried to protect her and killed the 'bad 'un' in revenge.

In another phantasy he showed that he had wishes to protect his father as well. One morning he went to his foster-mother several times to tell her long stories about his 'fairy' and his 'German'. At one point he had them together in a hole in the ground and was trying to guard them, becoming angry when Billy put sand into the hole, saying that his German would not like it. He had several fights with the German, and although once the German bombed the tractor he was driving (the garden roller) and smashed the brakes, on the whole Harry seemed to win. At lunch he said that his fairy had not come to him that night: 'I didn't let him; my burglar came instead.' The burglar, he said, was going to 'schlonk' him, but kissed him instead, 'because I wanted him to', after which he went back to the giant's house where he lived. In this phantasy Harry seemed as if he were trying to dramatize a good relationship between two people, which he himself could allow and protect from another child's interference (that is, from his own destructive wishes). The father, thus protected and with rights of his own, was a milder and more friendly figure, with whom Harry could have playful fights without being destroyed; in the same way, the burglar-father, who came when Harry voluntarily gave up the fairy-mother, kissed him instead of 'schlonking' him. Here again one saw his longing for a relationship with a loving and helpful father, as in his wish for his father to give him a sports car; but the unsympathetic attitude towards Harry which the father did, in fact, maintain, and his continued neglect of him, can only have confirmed his phantasies of a cruel, persecuting, revengeful father.

In the case of George (4), who had never known his father, the longing for a good, strong, protective father with whom he could be identified was very marked, as has been seen in his phantasies about Uncle Bill. George's mother made many complaints, in front of him, of his aggressive and destructive behaviour, more than once voicing doubts as to whether he would ever grow up into a 'nice man', while on one occasion she was considerably annoyed with him for not fitting a pair of trousers she had bought him, saying that she preferred tall, slim boys to short, stocky ones like George, and wondered if he was ever going to grow any bigger. She would seldom allow him to have the instruments of aggression he wanted: for instance, when he asked for a pistol, she gave him a musical box, and instead of the fire-engine he wanted, bought him an expensive mechanical ambulance, both of which he disliked from the first and quickly disposed of, smashing up the musical box and burying the ambulance in the garden. It was in his fury at being out first in a game that he went upstairs to his bedroom and destroyed his musical box, perhaps feeling that he was unable to win the game because he had been given something that was no use to him. On one occasion she did eventually give in to him and allow him to have the toy sword he had been badgering her to buy, but she fixed it in the scabbard so that he could not withdraw it, lest he should do damage with it. When George eventually managed to work the sword free, he flourished it so triumphantly that he cut another child on the finger, causing bleeding and tears. George was greatly upset; when the other child came into the room later, whimpering over his bandaged finger, George said in a consoling voice: 'I'll get another sword, Leslie, a big rubber one like grown-up boys have, and it won't hurt you.' Mrs. B. took charge of the sword, making clear that it was only for that evening, but George refused to have it back when it was offered to him the next day, and never asked for it again. It seems likely that the sword was, from the outset, bad because George had obtained it by forcing it out of his mother against her will, and because she had insisted that he would only hurt people with it. The whole situation must have confirmed George's phantasies of his own aggression—of having a bad, dangerous child's penis instead of the good constructive adult one he longed for, as represented in terms of swords by 'a big rubber one like grown-up boys have'.

While the boy has many anxieties about the nature of his masculinity, fearing it to be destructive and that he will be castrated as a punishment for aggressive activity, he has at least the reassurance of seeing that he still has a penis. The girl, on the other hand, has no evidence of her essential genital organs, and so in general her anxieties tend to be more widespread and her confidence less, although unconsciously she has an innate knowledge of her own sexual function. From an early age she seeks something from her father and wishes to take her mother's place in relation to him. This was seen clearly in the case of Dinah, who during her first three years showed a tendency to prefer her father and made efforts to oust her mother, remarking for instance: 'You go away in an aeroplane and I will marry Daddy.' As already suggested, the child's wishes for a relationship with one or other of his parents are felt to be implemented in his masturbatory activities, and in the case of the girl the excitement she experiences may in phantasy involve a hostile triumph over her mother. Sarah (4) went through a period when she would call to her mother at night and ask for cold cream because she was 'sore'. She always appeared rather distressed and guilty, and it seemed that she had to let her know about her activities, and that it was not only the soothing effect of the cream that she wanted, but also the reassurance that she was not angry, or shocked and reproachful. Her mother never scolded her, but suggested that it was rubbing herself that made her sore, and that she should not do it any more, and Sarah would then be able to go to sleep. When about nine years old, this same child would cry for her mother at night to tell her what a bad daughter she was to her, and would seem deeply upset, showing that the problem was still active, and suggesting that her need for her mother after masturbating was because of the injury she felt she had done to her. But although in phantasy the girl can feel at times that she succeeds in taking possession of the father, she is continually confronted with evidence to the contrary, and so feels herself to be the unsuccessful rival of her mother, who takes and keeps from her what she wants.

In her struggle to win the father's love, the girl has phantasies of robbing her mother in order to attract him, and the mother who is thus undermined comes to be seen as angry and retributive and is linked with the infant's earliest conception of a bad breast which starves and persecutes her. This terrifying phantasy mother is undoubtedly to some extent the basis of popular conceptions of witches and wicked step-mothers. For instance, Snow White's stepmother, as already suggested, shows her witch-like qualities in trying to kill the child when she feels robbed of her beauty by her. Kate described how, throughout her childhood, she would at times lie in bed at night, terrified to look up or move because she felt that a horrible witch was standing over the bed, waiting to pounce on her if she showed that she was alive or awake. Since, in reality, Kate's mother was depressed and often ill, and Kate was sometimes told by relatives that this was because she was so naughty, and there were angry scenes between her parents whenever her father wanted to take her out on his own, one might feel that the witch who came to kill her at night was perhaps the embodiment of her phantasy of a jealous, avenging, injured mother.

In the case of Eileen (5), rivalry with the mother was expressed partly by denial that she existed as a mother at all. Eileen was an only child, with loving and sympathetic parents. She was strongly attached to her father, and was abnormally shocked and upset when he was called into the army: she behaved as if she were his wife and in a deep depression, walking up and down, wringing her hands, and gazing at his photograph, while on Christmas Day she was only interested in his present to her, and refused food that she thought he would not be having. Shortly after he had gone, she distressed her mother very much by insisting that she was not her mother, but a kind lady who was looking after her, like those looking after the evacuees. The mother assured her that this was not so, and even offered to call in the doctor to testify that she really was her mother, but Eileen could not be convinced. Then the mother explained to her how she had been born, and how she, together with the father, had created her. Eileen was at once satisfied by this explanation, and able to recognize her again as mother. Soon after this the parents decided to have another child, an idea in which Eileen showed the greatest interest, with no apparent hostility or jealousy. She would ask whether her father was going to put in the seed on his next leave, and was always very much interested in his 'long thing', and the differences between him and her mother and herself. The mother accepted her curiosity and interest sympathetically, and answered all her questions quite naturally. Eileen seemed to become increasingly identified with her mother; during the mother's pregnancy she was always most concerned for her, helping her as an adult would and encouraging her to take care because of the little baby inside, while after it was born she was tender and loving towards it, and eagerly took responsibility for it. Eileen's behaviour seemed to be a dramatization of the phantasy that she could usurp her mother's role and take possession of her father. One can imagine that, in her father's absence, she not only lacked the reassurance of seeing with her own eyes that her parents were in fact a loving husband and wife, united to each other in spite of her wishes to interfere with and separate them, but also, in feeling like the bereft wife herself, was brought sharply face to face with an experience which she must have felt she had forced upon her mother in bereaving her. Her attitude of mourning for her father as if he were actually dead may have expressed a fear that in interfering with the parents' relationship she had killed him. Moreover, she may have felt anxious at being left alone to the mercy of a mother who, although in reality friendly and gentle, in phantasy had been attacked, and so could be expected to be angry and full of retaliation. In denying the relationship between herself and her mother, she was perhaps protecting them both from each other's attacks, but at the same time she was aggressively completing the displacement of her mother, and further severing the connection between her parents. Her ability to accept her mother again on being told the facts of the parents' sexual relationship must, in part, have sprung from the reassurance it gave her that she had not, after all, succeeded in doing this. The father's return on leave and the mother's subsequent pregnancy must have given further reassurance, while her unusual solicitude for her mother and her tenderness towards the new baby may well have been a compensation for her jealous and aggressive wishes. At the same time, her complete identification with her mother and her wish to know all the details of the baby's conception may have pointed to an undiminished need to be closely involved in the parents' relationship, and a persisting wish to take the mother's place.

In being so closely bound to the situation that she had to *become* her mother, Eileen was not free to be herself—a normal child. As the result of her guilt, a girl may be tied to her mother all her life, may suffer unnecessary concern over her mother's well-being, and may never feel able to leave home, or marry and have children of her own. This guilt, which has its seeds in infantile phantasies, is particularly acute in adolescence. Lily (13), whose mother was undergoing treatment in hospital for a chronic but not serious condition, was overwhelmed by feelings of remorse. Her life was arranged around telephone calls and visits to her mother, and she could not allow herself to be happy or to enjoy anything apart from her, having constantly to remind herself and everyone else of her mother's pain. Her school note-books were interspersed with such remarks as: 'My mother is a brave woman and suffers terribly, and I love her more than anybody else in the world', while the following is an extract from a letter to her mother in the hospital:

'I just can't wait to see you again Mummy darling. I like it very much here at Jean's . . . even if i do like it at Jean's I'd rather be with you I love you more than any person in the world you known that don't you. Don't let them hurt your bones will you hurry up and get better won't you don't worry about me will you i still think and worry about you please hurry up and get better. I think your the Prettiest and kind thoughtful genorise suffering woman in the world i will treat you better and do every think you say because you known best.'

Lily's parents had recently been divorced, and she was in her mother's care; although she evidently enjoyed going out with her father, with whom she had a good relationship, she could not acknowledge this, and had constantly to state that she loved her mother best and only wanted to be with her, and would describe how she had said so, when asked in the divorce court. It is likely that Lily's phantasies of having robbed and displaced her mother seemed confirmed for her by the divorce and by her mother's subsequent illness. Her unnecessary worry and alarm over her mother's condition and her need to protest so constantly that she loved her certainly seemed to point to guilt.

In the rivalry situation with the mother, the girl may feel extremely uncertain of the effectiveness of her own feminine powers, and this lack of confidence, together with her guilt and anxiety towards her mother, may result in a denial of her own femininity. Everyone is familiar with the tomboy stage through which so many girls pass, which generally occurs in middle childhood but sometimes persists into adolescence or adulthood. Many such girls and women consciously wish that they were boys or men, failure to be successfully feminine resulting in an over-estimation of the pleasures and powers of masculinity, while in some cases a girl may unconsciously feel that the only way to restore her mother is to become the father whom she has, in phantasy, stolen from her. On the other hand, the girl's anxiety about her femininity may result at all ages in exaggerated self-adornment and exhibitionism. Penelope (6) painted her toe-nails with red crayon, put pink chalk on her face, adorned herself with necklaces and ribbons, and indulged in much giggling and self-display. But this behaviour evidently did not convince her of her feminine status, as she openly said that she wished she had a penis, and at times would try to outdo the boys in noisy, reckless activities.

In both boys and girls we see an envy of the opposite sex and an anxiety about themselves. Both sexes often believe that the girl once had a penis which has already been cut off, and so she not only has not got one but is actually mutilated. Although 'girls don't have wee-wees' is often a remark of contempt made by small boys, it may also indicate anxiety, for if girls have had their penises cut off, there is always the possibility that the same might happen to boys. Moreover, boys also feel that they lack something unattainable. Christopher, at three, seemed to admire and to be mystified by the fact that his mother, unlike him, urinated sitting down on the lavatory, and several times remarked wistfully: 'I can't do wee-wee out of *my* bottom, can I!' One boy of five was puzzled and worried when told by his mother, in response to his questions, that he would never have milk nor bear babies, and tried to argue hopefully that men could, at least produce boy babies, while another boy of seven told his sister that he had milk in his chest, and had a drink at night whenever he felt thirsty. This was undoubtedly what he would have liked, since boys feel inferior as well as superior to girls, who have the power to make milk and babies, and whose genitals are hidden and therefore secret and mysterious.

In understanding something of the unconscious phantasies which children have about their parents and their own masturbatory activities, we may be more able to help them to grow up happily, and eventually to achieve adult sexual satisfaction themselves. A stable family background, with parents who stand united and cannot be turned against each other, is of the greatest importance to a child. He attributes significance even to minor disagreements: if, for instance, he knows that his father can be persuaded to allow him to do something which his mother has already forbidden, as in the case of Harry and Don, he has no reassurance that he cannot really come in between them, turn them against each other, and seduce one to his side at the expense of the other. Much can be done to mitigate the traumatic effects of separation due, for example, to war, illness, or death, if it is realized how great is the child's misplaced belief in the power of his own wishes. Because of his jealousy and hatred and his phantasies of violently separating and killing the parents or their substitutes, he may feel unconsciously that it is his fault if any separation should take place, although in reality it has been brought about by external factors. Hence, to try to spare a child grief by not talking about the absent parent can result in fostering a smouldering anxiety. The return of a parent who has been away for a considerable time may also be a difficult situation for the child, since he may have come to prefer being with one parent alone, and so feel displaced when again relegated to the position of a third person; he may also fear the retribution of the parent he had in phantasy successfully got rid of. The mother who does not mention the absent father and who lavishes all her affection and longing on the child (perhaps even to the extent of giving him his father's place beside her in the bed) risks increasing the child's anxiety both during the absence and at the return of his father.

If the child has, in reality, a good father and mother to identify with in a positive way, this helps to counteract jealous, hostile rivalry, and also to bring out the love feelings which are always there as well. When a boy has a father he can admire and copy, who will take him out, do things with him, show him how to make and build, and who, at the same time, can allow him to have an affectionate relationship with his mother without being jealous, he has a far greater chance of growing into a self-reliant, masculine person, who is confident that he can do constructive things. The mild, tolerant, friendly figure of his real father reassures him against the father from whom he feels he has stolen, and who is therefore either injured and powerless (and so causes him guilt), or angry and immensely terrifying and powerful. Similarly, if the little girl has a gentle, loving mother, who takes a pride in her, helps her to look attractive, and teaches her to do things with her, and who also shows that she does not feel injured or angry when the child does things with her father or appears to prefer his company, she is likely to be reassured against fears of being destructive and destroyed, and to feel certain, in identification with her mother, that she will one day be able to have a husband and babies herself. As we shall see in more detail in the last chapter, Dinah's good development during her first three years seemed in large part to be due to the fact that she had an easy-going and affectionate mother who was not perturbed by her rivalry and her preference, at times, for her father, but re-garded it all as a positive step forward. There were times when Dinah openly vied with her mother for her father's affection, but alongside these wishes to take her mother's place, there was a gradual acceptance of the real situation, and a growing conviction that she herself would be able to have a baby when she was a 'grown-up lady'.

With regard to the adult's attitude to masturbation, it is usually of most help to a child to show unconcern over it. If he emphatic-ally draws attention to it, it may be advisable to show that one is aware of it, since, on account of the terrifying phantasies which may accompany it, it can be very frightening, and the child may need support. In general, the way in which a child is helped to overcome anxieties about masturbation is primarily through a good relation with his parents, and through having evidence of a good relation between them, so that his fears of being able to interfere with and harm them are gradually modified. Also, when opportunity and encouragement are given to him to express his phantasies in varied and constructive ways, there is a decrease in anxiety and tension, which otherwise leads to further masturbation, in an attempt to gain reassurance and relief.

In giving sexual information, it seems wisest to answer all questions honestly as they arise, but not to force facts that are not wanted. Where the environment is free, curiosity will often be quite open, as in the case of Rose (8), who said to her aunt: 'Oh, do tell me all about hospitals; I'm *so* interested in bottoms, fronts and insides!' and to her father: 'Oh, you are lucky being a doctor; you must see *thousands* of bottoms!' Some children accept the information for the time being but soon forget it, as in the case of Charles (7), who was told by his mother clearly and without embarrassment the facts of his own birth, in response to his questions, but a few months later asked the same questions again, assuring her with the deepest conviction that she had never told him before. In many cases the truth is apparently accepted, but is distorted and confused by the child's own phantasies, so that even when, for instance, he has been told the facts of conception and birth, he may continue to believe that the mother is full of ready-made babies waiting to be born, that babies are made of food and faeces, or that they are born by way of the mouth or anus. A group of nursery school children were very much interested in the approaching birth of some guinea-pigs, and were told all about it. One day, however, Arthur (3) was seen holding the mother guinea-pig head downwards and gently squeezing her; he explained that he was sure the babies were ready to be born, but the mother would not spit them out. We have seen, too, how Dinah at 3.3 insistently maintained her theory of anal birth. In spite of such inevitable misconceptions, the value of giving a child accurate information about birth is shown in particular in the situation of the new baby. Colin, an only child, aged eight years, showed great anxiety when his mother told him that she was going to buy a baby, and from the first he was very hostile to the idea, saying fervently that he did not want any babies in the house. When the mother's abdomen began to increase in size, he would make gestures as if to punch it, and on several occasions did actually kick her, showing that he knew at least unconsciously where the baby was, although his mother had never told him. This child's general problems in relation to his mother were considerable, but he was very much relieved by being told the truth about her pregnancy, and became less hostile to the idea, saying that he would like to have a brother but not a sister, as a brother could play football with him. When, eventually, he did have a brother, he was not overpowered by his jealousy, and showed some positive feeling for him. The birth of a new baby may be a source of anxiety for a child, but it will also be a relief, particularly if he is an only child, as it can dispel his fears that he has done irreparable damage to his parents, and that his wishes to steal or kill their babies had taken effect.

In general, we see how very important infantile genital feelings are in a child's development, and how a mild, friendly attitude to him, genuine affection and sympathy and an honest answering of his questions can help to modify his terrifying phantasies in relation to them. When he has reached the point at which the genital is more important than the mouth and the anus as the centre of phantasy, the stage is set for development to normal adult sexuality. Moreover, parents or parent-substitutes play a vital part in furthering this development. When a child is allowed to take part in his parent's life, to work and play with them and to share their interests, he is reassured of his capacity to grow big like them, and of their willingness to allow him to grow up and marry and have children of his own, counteracting his fears that they will prevent him, which are dramatized in so many fairy tales in which the jealous parent tries to do away with the child before he is old enough to be a successful rival. Also, if his parents have a full life, he is reassured that his jealous wishes are not really taking effect, and that they are not injured and undermined by him. A child identifies himself not only with his parents as individuals, but bases his way of life, his attitudes and behaviour, his ideas of what is right and good, his standards of happiness, and the quality of his relationships, on theirs. To a very considerable extent, the eventual success of his own marriage depends upon his early experiences in his family.

CHAPTER SIX

Phantasy in Middle Childhood

As children grow older, we notice gradual but none the less striking changes in their interests, attitudes, and behaviour. The eight- or nine-year-old is largely concerned with activities that have definite, concrete results, with the exact ways in which things really work, and with rules, conventions, and accepted codes of behaviour—that is, with the world around him as it actually is. Bob (9), staying on a farm, was engrossed in watching and helping the men with their work, his conversation centring in the workings of agricultural machinery and details of farm management; Norman (8) was absorbed in making the practical arrangements for a secret society; while his sister Catherine (11) devoted all her energy to the acquiring of Girl Guide badges, and the planning of what she would need at camp.

Although at all ages the amount of phantasy expressed will depend to a considerable extent upon the environment, at this age it seems in general to be much less in evidence. This is partly due to some modification of it, as the child grows older, by increasing knowledge and experience of the real external world. The tiny child who screams with excitement and fear when a train passes cannot know that the engine is not something alive like himself, noisy, violent, and powerful as he would like to be, but is at the same time afraid of being, a creature whose behaviour is frighteningly unpredictable. The older boy, who makes lists of train numbers or sets out his model railway, knows more of the true nature of trains: he has learnt that they are under control and can only behave in certain ways. The dressing-gown which, to Harry, was a frightening object with a life of its own, jumping up and down in the night, the waste-pipe which seems to suck and gulp down the water like a greedy animal, and the coalman with his black face all lose their terror as the child discovers and is able to understand more of their real quality; and as they become less terrifying, they in their turn serve to modify the phantasy figures and objects which they represent.

In addition, there is in middle childhood an unconscious drive towards the repression of phantasy. At this stage there are often great efforts to overcome masturbation, largely in an attempt to escape from the guilt and fear arising from the under-lying phantasies—the dangerous and painful unfulfilled wishes to possess, displace, and separate the parents, which reached their height and were fully experienced at about three to four years. The child now deals with them by a gradual denial of the whole situation, which is seen in his growing reserve about emotional matters and his marked decrease in dependence on his parents, with some tendency to distrust them. Children of this age will often show embarrassment, contempt, or boredom over anything savouring of romantic or tender feeling, ashamed if their parents kiss them in front of their school-fellows, and even reluctant to be called by their Christian names if this is not the custom: for instance, Daphne (8) assured her mother when she visited her at her new boarding-school that parents were not allowed to take their children's arms. Paul (8) evinced a rooted objection to what he called 'love': he always expostulated over any intrusion of love interest in the films he saw, and if the wireless programme he was listening to included a 'love song', and the other people did not want to turn it off, he would make the maximum amount of protest, even stuffing his ears with newspaper in order to prevent himself from having to hear it. Several times he remarked vehemently that he disliked seeing couples sitting on the common, kissing each other and 'messing about'; he also drew a number of pictures of a man and woman, each labelled 'I don't lik luv' or 'luv is soppy'.

The feelings of love and hate which in early childhood were expressed vividly and directly towards the parents are now canalized and socialized, and seen in relation to other adults, as for instance in admiration of famous men and women, real or fictional, and later of Scout-masters and games mistresses, and in contempt for villains, unsuccessful school-teachers, and all people on 'the wrong side'. The external world, with its comparatively stable limits, its emphasis on control and conformity, and its recognized moral standards, offers safety and reassurance against the incalculable, uncontrollable, and often overwhelming inner world of phantasy.

From this it might look as if, in middle childhood, phantasy is no longer an integral part of the child's personality. There is, however, evidence that it is not only operative, but is, in fact, finding expression in reality terms. Many of the interests of seven- to eleven-year-old children, although strongly tied to reality, can be seen to be deeply rooted in phantasy. For instance, Paul (8) would periodically spend days digging in the garden to find buried treasure—'jewels' and 'olden-day things'. He dug up several pieces of china, which he carefully washed and tried to fit together, convinced that they were fragments of ancient pottery and probably of great value, and eager to present them to a museum; he also found a ring, which he insisted should be taken to a jeweller to be valued, and was delighted to find worth thirty shillings. At other times he was busy digging a tunnel in an attempt to find a secret passage into the house, and tapping walls and exploring the boxroom to try to find the other end of it, certain that it must exist. As already described, in trying to find his lost mouth-organ he thought of digging in the garden for it in case it had got buried, and in so far as this object seemed to stand for some good thing belonging to his mother, one might take his repeated searches for hidden valuables to express a phantasy of digging into her body ('Mother Earth'), 'jewels' and 'treasure' perhaps representing the penises and babies he expected to find inside her, and 'olden-day things' the good breast which he had long ago possessed, and now like the mouth-organ had lost. Similarly, his many efforts to find an underground passage into the house could be seen as the acting-out of a phantasy of seeking a secret way into the mother—secret in so far as it was not known consciously by Paul himself, and possibly, too, because he felt it to belong to someone else. Other material, which will be discussed later, pointed to Paul's deep interest in the contents of the human body, to his desire, combined with horror, to look inside it, and to his equation of all acts of enquiry and investigation with an aggressive penetration of the mother and a displacing of the father.

This element of secrecy and its relation to underlying phantasy is seen particularly in the organization of gangs, with their secret languages, signs, and meeting-places, and exploits and activities which must be hidden from the adults even if, in reality, they would be approved of and permitted. Here the tables are turned: the child himself has an exciting alliance with other children from which his parents are debarred. In the secret society organized by Norman, there was some evidence of the underlying sexual meaning of that alliance. Each child who wished to become a member had to walk along a high wall without falling off, to refrain from crying when salt was rubbed into a pinprick made in the arm, and to show that he or she possessed at least one pubic hair. While the third condition clearly showed the desirability in Norman's mind of being sexually mature, the other two, signifying active physical prowess and passive endurance of pain, may possibly have expressed phantasies of masculine and feminine roles in intercourse. Here, as in the case of Paul, the disguise of phantasy certainly did not lead to a less graphic expression of it.

Apart from giving powerful support against the adults and the gratification of a rival alliance, a gang allows a child opportunity to express primitive feelings of love and hate in the approved and more socialized sphere of trusty comrades and sworn enemies—feelings which, basically, belong to his parents and brothers and sisters. In the same way, games and activities of all kinds in which there is rivalry give legitimate outlet to aggressive and exhibitionistic impulses which, at this age, can generally no longer be brought out into the open and expressed directly.

For instance, in the popular games of chance which are played with such tireless enthusiasm, the child can in winning be enacting his wishes to steal and displace, exploit and triumph, while in losing he can feel robbed, cheated, and punished, yet all the time with the reassuring knowledge that the result has been achieved solely by the rules and luck of the game. Athletics and games involving physical activity serve as proofs of what the individual can do with his body, thus reassuring the child that he is whole and strong and potent; they, too, allow expression of aggressive impulses and, in permitting effortful use of the body to its full extent, must give particular relief from the fight against masturbation, with its demand for rigid control and inactivity. Some activities, such as wrestling, boxing, pillow-fights, tickling games, and horseplay of all kinds give direct gratification of the wish for physical contact, which was expressed in early childhood in cuddling, riding on the parent's knee, and being given pick-a-back rides. In Vera (9) one saw something of the value of a particular physical activity as an outlet for aggressive and sexual impulses. Vera had spent most of her life in an enemy-occupied country, where, although she apparently encountered no actual cruelties, there was inevitably an atmosphere of hatred and oppression. Her mother was fundamentally selfish and dominating, insisting on instant obedience, and criticizing Vera continually;

at the same time, she denied herself food in order that Vera should have enough, and finally became ill. Some months after they had settled in England, Vera was sent to a co-educational boarding school. Here she wore a mask of politeness and docility and seemed anxious to placate and ingratiate herself with the adults, but she made no real contact with anyone, and stole and lied, was slyly disobedient, and secretly cruel to younger children. Her play was very limited, and consisted mainly of rough games in which other children often got hurt, while her only efforts to be constructive lay in the careful, meticulous painting, over and over again, of a beautifully decorated, stylized ship, peopled with tiny, black, active figures. Her particular form of amusement was to play frightening or annoying practical jokes on other people, jumping out at them from behind doors in the dark, hiding on top of the wardrobe and leaping on to children who were in bed, and hiding their clothes and possessions; she would also terrify those in her dormitory by telling them stories about witches and ghosts. As time went on, however, Vera made a contact with the games master and, with his encouragement, began to be very much interested in running. She would spend all her free time running round and round the cricket pitch trying to beat her own record, while he timed her with a stop-watch. The more energy and enthusiasm Vera put into her running, the less sadistic her relationship with other children grew. It seems as if through her good relationship with this master, involving a satisfying physical experience, she was able to achieve something constructive, and was less compelled to enact scenes of bodily attack.

Many phantasies are expressed by children in the middle years in terms of their possessions. In some children there is an exaggerated dependence on external objects, as in the case of Tony, who, because he could never face grief at having destroyed something, had either to turn from the damaged object and quickly make reparation in relation to something or someone else, or to direct his attention to some longed-for, idealized object, unable to rest until he had gained possession of it. His interest in the episode in *The Snow Queen*, in which Kay is promised 'the whole world and a new pair of skates' if he can solve the ice puzzle, suggests that Tony felt the need to acquire something perfect and all-satisfying, which would make him omnipotent. When his schoolteacher read the story of *The Fisherman and his Wife* to her class and asked some of the children what they would choose if they could have one wish granted, Tony promptly said: 'The whole world', adding that then he would own every-thing, and everyone else's wishes would be useless. Another favourite story of his was *The Tinder Box*: he never seemed to tire of discussing what one could obtain by means of such a box, and was full of admiration for the soldier's ruthless acquiring of it. But in practice he seemed so deeply convinced that to possess anything was to destroy it, that as soon as he had obtained the object he had set his heart on he seemed compelled to break it. To Jill (7), on the contrary, external objects, far from being idealized, seemed of little value. She was an unloved child who at school gave the picture of an empty and aimless personality. She seemed to crave for contact and went from one teacher to another, clinging to each of them but unable to make a stable relationship of any depth. Material objects of all kinds seemed to hold for her no absolute value in themselves, but were used or misused to gain attention or to create an exciting situation, to be discarded without hesitation or apparent regret when they no longer served such a purpose. Jill gave away all her toys at school in an attempt to buy friendship, and would sometimes force another child to accept something he did not want, and then try to get him accused of 'stealing' it. She would damage her own clothes or possessions and blame another child, as for instance on the occasion when she threw her own pocket-money out of the window, and then tried to prove that a younger child had done it. If her teacher tried to help her to take care of her things and to encourage her to feel proud of them and of herself, she would at first respond, but with an air of simply wishing to please; inevitably, sooner or later, she would manage to dispose of everything, as when, a week after her birthday, she announced with evident satisfaction that she had not one present left intact. Many phantasies must have lain behind this repeated pattern of behaviour, it being clear that in her attitude to her possessions Jill was expressing feelings about herself and her inner life. Her urgent need to get rid of them suggests that they were not only felt to be without value, but positively dangerous; perhaps, in making contact with them at all, she had damaged them and made them bad, while, in so far as they represented the people of her internal world, she may have felt that they were so badly injured by being taken inside her that they must immediately be thrown out again, the extent of her guilt about her destructiveness being shown in her determination that someone should be blamed and punished for it. In the same way, new relationships had constantly to be made and then broken off almost immediately, as if to show that Jill herself was too worthless and dangerous a person for anyone to keep; in fact, it seemed as if she had repeatedly to throw herself out of the window, along with her pocket-money. In general, however, great importance is attached at this age to possessions, collections of all kinds being constantly added to, reorganized, and improved; carelessly lost, spoilt, or exposed to dangers; anxiously retrieved and repaired, or mourned over; and eventually abandoned for something unquestionably better.

As in collecting, so in making and doing, much satisfaction is experienced at this age. In being practical and constructive, a child can give expression to his good impulses, and gain reassurance as to their power. He does this in many different ways, as for instance in building and equipping a camp, knitting a kettle-holder, picking blackberries, and cleaning out the rabbits. In a Children's Home a favourite occupation was making tarts, the most enjoyable part of this being the moment when they were proudly handed round to everyone in the house. With these children one saw the value of allowing and enabling them to 'make good' in their own individual ways and as the need arose. Laura (8) would decide to give the house a 'good clean-up', even though it might have just been cleaned; William (6) would sometimes choose to spend a morning clearing up the garden and burning the rubbish, taking delight in the hardships and difficulties of the situation, and being quite unmoved by rain; Elizabeth (10) felt that the grown-ups should have early-morning tea in bed, and got up regularly to make it; Clive (11) took on the bathing of Dicky (22 months) when his mother was out, and treated him with the greatest tenderness and care, requesting 'proper' baby soap, and himself buying talcum powder; Nancy (9), although rather ineffectual and unreliable in general, found success and satisfaction in collecting nature specimens and arranging them for everyone to see. In all these instances, one saw how responsibility was welcomed by the children, and that they gained in skill and confidence as the result of it.

Learning and school work too, have their underlying phantasy meanings as well as their conscious significance. As already seen in Chapter III, the figures of speech used about learning suggest that it is a taking-in process which is related, amongst other things, to the early feeding situation. Generally in the case of young children learning centres in the teacher-pupil relationship, a teacher's ability to give out good material and to stimulate and satisfy the children under her care being as unconsciously meaningful to her as to the children themselves. At the same time, the relationship of the child with his work has the significance of a feeding situation, quite apart from his relationship with his teacher, the learner always feeling that he is taking from and giving to somebody, even when working independently. We know how adults can feel that work thrusts itself upon them, reproaching them if left unfinished and rewarding them if they have given time and energy to it, implying the existence of a give-and-take relationship. In its deepest meaning, this is a relationship with inner phantasy figures, which are projected on to the work, so that the problems of love and hate are enacted in it. As we have seen, the basis of a satisfactory feeding situation is the child's feeling that in taking in good things in a loving way he makes his mother good, and that with what he is given he is able to create something of value. Learning can in many ways be a means of reparation; on the other hand, it may be invested with meanings of attack and destruction, often resulting in inhibition and failure. Some children are receptive and creative and take an active part in the learning process; in others, interest and curiosity do not lead to gain in knowledge or skill in spite of normal intelligence, facts being confused with each other or quickly forgotten, explanations half-heard or interrupted with irrelevant remarks; while yet others may appear to take in knowledge and to accept facts and principles, but are not able to make use of them, often with the hopeless attitude that no work they produce can ever be any good.

In the case of Paul (9), already referred to, many phantasies seemed to lie behind his severe learning inhibition. Paul had always disliked going to school, and while still living with his mother often complained that he did not feel well in the morning, with the result that he was allowed to stay in bed. When he first went to live with his governess in the country, after the divorce, he was sent to the village school, as it was felt that he needed to mix with other children, but he made so many protests and did so badly there that eventually it was recommended that he should stay at home and be taught by his governess instead. To begin with she felt that Paul would be a pleasure to teach, as he was highly intelligent and had always shown a lively interest in what was going on around him. He was very much interested in scientific matters—in the way things were made and worked, in what happened to things under different conditions (as, for example, in chemical experiments), and in the workings of the mind and body. He would discuss the motives of human behaviour, would ponder over such questions as why people laugh when something is funny, and was easily able to grasp the explanation of a psychologist, in reply to his enquiry as to what her work was, that she was concerned with the ways in which people thought and felt, and why they did so. He liked to look at diagrams of human and animal anatomy, to consider the functions of various organs, and to know where different vessels led to; he was also interested in maps, particularly those which showed the position of buried treasure or a secret island, while, as already discussed, he was concerned with the whole subject of treasure-seeking. On occasions when one of his pet rabbits died, or the cat brought in a dead bird, Paul, having first shown regret, would ask for it to be dissected in order to see what was inside it, reassuring himself that it could no longer feel and so could not be hurt.

In spite of such keen interests, however, Paul seldom went far beyond the stage of initial enquiry. He would ask for explanation of a diagram, but after a few seconds his attention would wander, and the point would not be reached. Although his teaching at home was largely based on his interests, it was not successful; for instance, although he seemed interested in maps he hated to have to draw one, even when unhampered by directions and left free to invent, and his productions were surprisingly unimaginative and inept. Having watched a chemical experiment and obviously understood the purpose and process, he would afterwards be unable to relate what had happened, and generally his attempts to express in writing an idea or fact were failures.

This disability was in marked contrast to his conversational powers, since in discussions he could put quite complicated and difficult ideas into words with clarity. He also had a great aversion to arithmetic; he found it impossible to remember the simplest process, although he had shown that he understood it, while tables learnt by heart were useless to him when it came to working out a sum. He seemed particularly to dislike having to do calculations on paper in any given manner, and always preferred to do them in his head, producing an answer which was generally nowhere near the right one. It became clear that Paul's keen interests were being considerably limited by his inability to take in or make practical use of what was offered. In every branch of learning he was inattentive and forgetful, constantly interrupting his teacher or his own work to discuss something other than the matter in hand, and even when the subject was one in which he had shown a deep interest, he would often confuse or reduce to nonsense information which he had shown eagerness to have.

It seemed as if part of Paul's problem was a need to deny his own curiosity, to avoid facing the results of it, and an inability to allow himself to gain what he wanted from it. This denial was seen particularly in relation to what he called 'love': in spite of his avowed disgust at lovers on the common, his underlying curiosity was unmistakable, since he seemed compelled to go on looking at them, while his protests against love songs on the wireless resulted in the maximum attention being drawn to them. His disgust clearly pointed to a feeling that what the lovers were doing was bad, as was perhaps also expressed in his picture illustrating the statement 'I don't lik luv', in which a man was kissing a woman who was singing, with the words 'Smack! Smack!' issuing from his mouth. Moreover, his emphatic denials that he was in fact looking and listening might indicate that these very acts themselves seemed bad, and this was further suggested when, in discussing the work of a doctor, he remarked with horror: 'Ugh! I should hate to be a doctor and cut open ladies' bodies and see inside them!' looking into thus involving attack. That ladies' bodies stood in Paul's mind specifically for his mother's body was shown by the fact that he immediately went on to talk of an operation his mother had undergone, saying that 'something went wrong inside her'. In addition, the penetration and investigation of her seemed, as already discussed, to be a phantasy underlying his treasure-seeking games. Perhaps it was because this act of curiosity seemed basically so aggressive and destructive that every investigation came to mean to him something dangerous, representing both an interfering prying and a cruel sexual attack. In his guilt and shame he had constantly to try to conceal what he felt he was doing: to prove that he had not been watching or listening by not remembering what he had seen or heard, to avoid demonstrating in writing what he had found out, and to hide away in his head the means whereby he reached the thing he sought, as for instance the working of a sum.

It is likely that Paul's infantile phantasy of a destructive sexual relationship had seemed to some extent confirmed for him by the facts of his parents' divorce. Although at times he could appreciate intellectually that it was the mother who was divorced, he generally maintained that it was not she who was to blame, and felt bitterly towards his father for, as he felt, cruelly and unreasonably rejecting her, thus seeing it as a situation in which the father was attacker and the mother his victim. Paul had also been distressed and indignant over his father's refusal, after the divorce, to let him see his mother, who was still living in the same part of London; this had led to his defying him by meeting her secretly in the streets on his way home from school, with the result that his father became for him someone who forced him into an illicit relationship with the mother, and at the same time threatened to punish him for it. Thus to investigate and take possession of the mother was doubly dangerous, for not only was it in itself an aggressive and destructive activity, but it incurred the jealousy and anger of the father.

It was this phantasy, reawakened and coloured by the current situation, which Paul seemed to be enacting in his relationship with school and learning. In the days when he went to school, he constantly complained that the headmaster caned children for offences they had not committed, and blamed them when it was really someone else's fault, and was bitterly indignant when he himself was punished for a lie which, he said, the headmaster had tricked him into telling. When later Miss R. became his teacher, her role for him changed: he began to see her less as someone understanding and sympathetic, who even in her appearance reminded him of his mother, and more as a harsh father-figure who forced him into aggressive and dangerous activity, so much so that he one day remarked angrily: 'You never did really like me!' In so far as she seemed to be attacking him in trying to make him learn, he had to defend himself and attack back, and so, in addition to being slow, unpunctual, and forgetful, he was disobedient, and lied and cheated over his work. At the same time there were certain changes in his general behaviour, and apparently in his personality. Hitherto he had shown concern over any form of violence, and had himself been particularly gentle, sensitive, and passive, perhaps partly in an attempt to bring to life an unharmed mother by becoming her, as well as to avoid rivalry with his father. Now he grew rough and noisy and dangerously destructive, and had frequent 'accidents' in which things were broken and the children he played with were hurt, generally maintaining an attitude of irresponsibility and indifference, in which he would try to shift the blame on to someone else.

One day he remarked reproachfully to his governess: 'I seem to have changed; I seem to be a different boy now.' Here, although from his tone of voice he seemed to imply that it was really she who was responsible for his change, and to be wanting to cut himself off from the aggressive part of himself, his underlying guilt could be detected. It was perhaps further suggested by the violence of his reaction when his cat killed a bird: each time this happened he was overcome with horror and grief, not only because he himself was unable to save or heal the bird, but because he had to accept that it was the cat's nature to destroy in this way—a fact which he questioned and railed against in the same way in which he repeatedly discussed the subject of his parents' divorce: 'Why did it *have* to happen?' In his effort to convince himself that it was the bad teacher who had made him into 'a different boy', he unsuccessfully tried to lay on her the blame for the destruction resulting from his aggression; similarly, in consistently blaming his father for the divorce, he was perhaps trying to avoid facing the feeling that it was really he who had been responsible for it, as an inevitable sequel to the phantasy of prying into the parents' sexual life and himself taking possession of the mother. An underlying urge to punish himself was no doubt one of the elements dramatically expressed in situations of self-destruction and injury. Whereas he had, in the past, discussed theoretically the possibilities of suicide—how easy it would be to fall under a train; whether the bread knife would be sharp enough to cut one's throat with—he now enacted such ideas. For instance, he climbed recklessly to the top of a tall tree from which he could not get down except by throwing himself most of the way, and on one occasion he was found with a rope round his neck and over a branch, preparing, as he said, to try to pull himself up into the tree that way, while he frequently bruised and scratched himself, crashed into anyone or anything that lay in his path when he rode his scooter, and behaved in reckless and forbidden ways with fire.

These changes in Paul seemed to have their centre in the fact that his governess became his teacher, but at the same time there were a number of other factors in his environment which were no doubt contributory. During the preceding summer he had spent an unsuccessful and unhappy holiday with his father and stepmother, and had once again been forbidden to see his mother, who was still living in the same part of London. He met her one day in the street, however, without his father's knowledge, and was filled with renewed guilt and fear. Another disturbing factor, on his return to the country, was the presence of his grandfather who had come down for a month's fishing. Paul had always been somewhat antagonistic towards him, and during the difficult period which followed the visit to London showed considerable anxiety over the fact that his grandfather could not control him, nor prevent his aggressive acts. At this time, too, Paul started having weekly treatment at a Child Guidance Clinic, and it seemed possible that the long interval between each session helped to increase his anxiety.

In turning to Paul's special difficulties in school subjects, one may find some indication of the particular phantasies which determined them. His marked dislike of arithmetic was probably not only because in his disturbed state he was unable to concentrate, but also because of an identification of it with masculinity, shared by many. That in general boys are better at mathematics than girls is often said to depend on basic differences in the masculine and feminine minds, such as reasoning power and capacity for objectivity, but these differences in themselves might be seen to be the product of underlying phantasies. For instance boys, having external evidence that they are sexually complete, may feel freer to turn to impersonal outside things in an objective way than girls, whose essential organs are hidden and in phantasy may be missing, while the fact that mathematics demand open display of proof, the answer often not being accepted without it, may for the same reason cause the girl to feel at a disadvantage. To Paul, however, masculinity implied an aggressive and destructive activity, and a dangerous rivalry with the father.

As already suggested, his dislike of writing perhaps sprang, in part, from his wish to avoid revealing in black and white the bad thing he felt he was doing, or had done. It is also possible that the act of writing, in itself, was felt by him to be aggressive and destructive: he often talked about his 'bad writing' and pointed out how, when he wrote with ink, the result was 'all messed up'. It may be interesting to note the few occasions on which Paul wrote voluntarily, or with resulting satisfaction. Once was in the moment of relief and renewed love for his governess after the restoration of the mouth-organ, when he wrote a reminder to himself to turn off the light, as she had asked, thus using writing as a means of pleasing her and of showing that he was a constructive and not a destructive person. There was also the occasion when he wrote 'I don't lik luv' as an interpretation of his picture of two lovers, thereby denying in writing his interest in adult sexuality. One other piece of writing was done with willingness and more fluency than usual; having been asked in his lessons to show the use of the words 'amazed', 'advised', and 'encouraged', he produced, with unmistakable satisfaction: 'I was amazed to here that sukey had sum mor kittens and I advise her not to but the tom cats encurag her.' Here again he was condemning sexual relations, at the same time as showing his concern with them.

His persistent bad spelling, which showed no improvement in spite of intelligence, a good visual memory, and the maximum amount of direct help, was probably due in part to his obstinate resistance to his teacher, as even when she gave him words to copy into his notebook, he would write them down incorrectly. But beyond this, Paul's repeated misspelling of the same words might suggest an unconscious wish to mutilate them, perhaps with the feeling that if he were forced to write (that is, in his own mind, to attack), the result could only be something damaged. In particular, he seemed to be genuinely confused as to where to put the terminal 'e', and in spite of many lessons on the subject invariably wrote such things as 'saide' and 'hav'. At the village school he had attended for a short while, it was called 'the magic e', and its use explained to the children in terms of doing something mysterious and important to a word when added. In view of Paul's anxieties about sexuality, his confusion could point to an underlying doubt as to who should have the extra thing—the powerful magic penis. It could apply to Paul himself, expressing both an attempt to be feminine rather than aggressively masculine, and a fear that his father would castrate him in revenge for his relationship with his mother; it could also be seen as his wish to steal the penis from the father, or, in line with his phantasy of valuable things being inside the mother's body, might suggest an unconscious belief that in intercourse the father's penis is retained there. In forming letters and figures, there was, too, real confusion in Paul's mind as to which way round they faced, while in learning cursive writing he had great difficulty in remembering which letters joined at the top and which at the bottom. Paul himself volunteered no clue as to what these particular difficulties meant to him, but one might feel that confusion as to which was the front and which the back of a figure and as to whether a letter made contact with the next in one way or another could relate to doubt about the nature of sexual relationships, especially in view of the double meaning of the word 'figure'. As a result of his many mistakes and mis-corrections, Paul's written work often ended by being a mass of blots, smudges, and obliterations, as if writing were something in which he could take no pride and pleasure, but rather, in his eyes, a dirty and shameful business.

In Paul we get some indication of the complexity of phantasy which underlies the learning of school subjects—an activity which might, on the surface, appear to be entirely governed by reality values. In his case, anxiety about sadistic wishes led to his being unable to learn, although he had a lively conscious wish to know; in others the inhibition of curiosity leads to boredom and apathy. But to the majority of children learning is, on the whole, a positive activity, expressing constructive phantasies. As a rule, a child feels that school work well done is something good, and so is reassured about his own potency and power to repair, while many anxieties are allayed by knowledge about real things. Moreover, all children make use of the school situation, in itself, as a setting outside home in which they can express phantasies in terms of parent-figures who are not parents, and other children who are not brothers and sisters.

Above all, phantasy is expressed in imaginative play, although in middle childhood this tends to be less free than in early years, when it occurs spontaneously, with whatever material comes to hand. Although children of this age do many constructive things on their own, their imaginative play usually occurs in groups. Whereas the little child makes much use of toys and other materials to play out his phantasies, as he grows older he depends more and more in his imaginative games on the co-operation of other children playing different roles, and acting as a support to him in expressing phantasies more directly and overtly than in other forms of activity. The imaginative games of an older child are generally formalized to some extent, and are often carefully planned in advance, while there is frequently an insistence that they should be played with real materials, and that the setting should be true to life. But in spite of this limiting of imagination by adherence to reality, which must surely be partly due to a fear of underlying phantasies, these are expressed both in the situations the children choose to depict and the way they carry them out. In the school and hospital games, for instance, generally played by girls, the relationship between teacher and pupil, nurse and patient, must often represent the child's phantasy of a mother-child relationship. In boys' games of pirates, Indians, cowboys, gangsters, or simply 'good 'uns and bad 'uns', the implied if not actual presence of an enemy is an essential part of the game, and plotting ways to outwit them, overhearing their plans, stealing their ammunition or supplies, shooting or capturing them, can be seen to symbolize the child's wish to overpower and replace his father. The very strict teacher with her favourites, the rude and cheating pupil, the dominating, over-attentive nurse, the patient in extreme pain, the angry, retributive enemy, and the numerous other roles that are played, are all representatives of the child's phantasy figures.

Many phantasies of putting right, restoring, and repairing are expressed in imaginative play. Bob (8) was genuinely worried by his habit of lying, saying hopefully: 'I'm getting a bit better about telling lies, aren't I?' One day he built what he called a church in the garden and put his Bible in it, saying that only people who spoke the truth could be admitted. One of his games was called *Swallows and Amazons*, based on the book by Arthur Ransome in which he had been particularly interested. With one or two younger children, to whom he behaved in a kindly, parental way, he would build and equip a boat in which they were to sail to an unknown island. They never reached the stage of setting sail, however, the whole point of the game lying in the preparations and the loading up of the boat with every conceivable object which might be needed on the journey and for camping. It seems likely that both the church and the boat stood for his mother (cf. the term 'Mother Church', and the fact that boats are always referred to in feminine terms and are often given female names). The putting of the Bible in the church and the equipping of the boat could mean restoring the mother by putting good things inside her, and by preventing the entrance of bad things—people who tell lies. Also, the fact that Bob played the part of a mother to the younger children would suggest that he was at the same time building up himself, and that in incorporating the Bible, he was taking in something strong and good which could control his bad impulses, represented by his lying. Many imaginative games of hospitals with sick patients and careful, devoted nurses, and of mothers and babies, express this wish to make reparation, and much satisfaction is gained from dressing the patient's wounds and making him comfortable, feeding and changing the baby, and being the good person on whom people depend. Shop games can express many different phantasies, the shopkeeper sometimes having everything in stock and taking pleasure in pleasing his customers, like the mother overflowing with good things, and sometimes frustrating them by repeatedly not having what is wanted. Bob was always most polite to the people in his shop, but would tell them with a beaming smile that he was very sorry that the shop had 'wasted out of' what they asked for.

Sometimes the imaginative play of older children takes the form of spontaneous acting; for instance, Joan (9), with the help of friends from school who had come to tea, once got up a play called 'The Horrid Little Boy' in which she herself took the part of an intolerant and domineering mother with several children. The youngest, Benny, was continually scolded and mocked by her and the father and by the other children for his bad behaviour, and was eventually sent to live in the dog kennel and given nothing to eat but an old bone, while the dog Twister was given his bed and his place at the table, and was patted and caressed. At Christmas, Father Christmas brought all the children presents, but, under the instructions of the mother, gave Benny nothing. In the last scene (announced as 'Where they discover the mother is a princess'), at Joan's instigation—she told the actors exactly what to do, step by step—the children rose up against the mother while she slept, peeped at her though the keyhole, took all her treasures out of her jewel box, and went to her drawers and read her letters, in which they found her name written down. When the mother woke and found that she had been cheated and robbed, she flew into a rage and tried to imprison the children in a tower, but they were too strong and drove her off. In the end she was left alone on the stage, crying; she called the dog, saying that he was the only friend she had left in the world, and walked off slowly and sadly. This play is particularly interesting in view of Joan's own history. She was the sister of Harry, and so also experienced a depressed and neglectful mother who eventually deserted her and was not seen again. The father often voiced to the children feelings of bitterness and resentment about his wife, and Joan seemed convinced that she had a very bad mother, as was shown by the treatment of Benny, and also by stories she told on various occasions of how her mother had threatened to drown Harry, and how she, Joan, had saved him by her protests. What came out so clearly in the play, however, was Joan's underlying sense of responsibility about her mother's desertion. The very convincing and sympathetic performance which she gave of the mother, sad and alone, suggested her deep feeling of guilt and remorse over her own wicked behaviour, represented by the children's reading of the letters and stealing of the jewels, which drove the mother away. Moreover, since the fact of the mother's being a princess was kept a secret from the children in the play, one might infer that Joan herself had a secret picture of a good, rich, beautiful mother, very different from the depressed and neglectful real mother, and that it was this good mother who was made unhappy by the children's attacks, and eventually driven away. In this way Joan seemed to show that she felt responsible not only for her mother's desertion, but also for her depression.

Tony (8) vividly dramatized certain phantasies in a wedding play. It was to celebrate the birthday of Arthur, the billet-mother's brother, was performed in her bedroom, and only the two of them were allowed to see it. He induced two younger children who lived nearby to play the parts of king and queen, his role being to control and dictate all their activities. For the wedding ceremony, the bridal pair walked through an arch made by Tony and the billet-mother, temporarily enlisted. After the wedding he photographed them with a bicycle lamp, having carefully arranged them in suitable positions holding flowers. He then tucked them up in a coach with pillows and blankets, and, as a statue on the procession route, stood motionless while they drove past him. The drive was followed by a wedding feast of real food, which was held in the dark by the light of one candle, with Tony, usually greedy, denying himself a single mouthful, but directing exactly what the married couple should eat and give to each other, and encouraging them to finish everything up. After the feast there was an entertainment, the king and queen sitting still on the floor while Tony did a strange, monotonous, shuffling dance in front of them, movement being strictly limited to the feet. In this illuminating game, Tony seemed to be dramatizing a phantasy that he could control the sexual activities of the parents (perhaps represented currently by Arthur and the billet-mother), while admitting at the same time that this was far from the truth. The coach was clearly intended as a bed, while the drive and the feast could be taken to symbolize intercourse in which he could play no part. Tony's own role was that of a dominating figure who permitted and organized their enjoyment, and who, by proving himself to be superior, avoided the pain of envy. On the other hand he was a stone statue, lifeless and fixed and powerless to do anything as the couple drove by, suggesting that he knew he could do nothing in reality to enter the relationship, but could only watch, paralysed. The fact that his phantasy of controlling was an attempt to deny feelings of inferiority and impotence was shown by his very poor, ineffectual, and solitary dance, which may possibly have represented an unsatisfying attempt to share the parents' pleasure by means of masturbation.

Another marriage play, based on a recent royal wedding, was acted by two girls of eight and nine years. As prince and princess they went behind a screen to get married, immediately sending for coffee to drink. On the way out the prince called for beer, and they then went straight home to bed (a sofa) and ordered fish and chips. The prince made a wireless and gave it as a wedding present to the princess, who turned it on, after which they both went to sleep for a few minutes, waking up 'next morning'. A three-year-old child had been hidden under the blankets, and was now told to emerge from the bottom of the bed as the baby prince who had just been born. A cot was made for him out of two arm-chairs, and his father's crown was put on his head. There was then a squabble as to whose child he was, the princess saying: 'He's my baby—I had him', and the prince replying indignantly: 'Well, after all, *I'm* his father!' The play ended gaily with the prince's going off for a ride on the rocking-horse. Here, too, the sexual meaning is manifestly clear: intercourse is again represented by eating and drinking, while the processes of impregnation and conception are dramatized in the making, giving, and turning on of the wireless, followed so quickly by the birth of a child.

It is at this age, particularly, that phantasy finds vivid expression in fairy stories, which, terrifying and horrible as they sometimes may be, act as a relief in representing in a modified form phantasies still more terrifying, and give assurance that goodness overcomes wickedness. Within a stable framework of reality, and with increasing ability to perceive and hold fast to the more consistent values of the external world, the normal child experiences a rich imaginative life. For an example of a child's satisfaction in reality, side by side with pleasure in imagination, we might consider Lewis Carroll's picture of Alice, based on a real little girl, who begged for stories and delighted in games of 'let's pretend', and at the same time found security in the rules and conventions of a Victorian upbringing. Both in *Wonderland* and *Through the Look-*

ing Glass the adults are drawn as far more childish than Alice herself: they are quarrelsome, tearful, unreasonable, messy, careless, forgetful, and jealous, while Alice, although at times worried, frightened, or dismayed, never loses sight of reality, and is full of sound advice and common sense. They could be taken to represent her former babyish self—an Alice whose behaviour as a little child could only have been impulsive and based largely on phantasy, in contrast to that of the seven-year-old Alice, firmly established in the world of reality, where things are consistent and reasonable and orderly. Her disgust at the bad manners of the Mad Hatter and his friends and her exasperation at their muddled arguments are surely influenced by the fact that not so long ago she, too, must have been childish in these ways, while her attitude to the White Queen who makes such a fuss over a pricked finger and even cries before she is hurt, to the Knight who is clumsy and muddle-headed, and to the gardeners whose quarrels are so petty, all point to this contrast between the infant and the older child. If from one point of view we like to read this story as an allegory, we can see in Alice the fulfilment of every child's wish to be sane and reasonable and grown-up, and to be identified with the stable values of the real world. There are, however, moments in the two dreams when the creatures of her infantile phantasies threaten to overpower her, and necessitate her strongly denying their existence and waking up; for instance at the end of *Through the Looking-Glass*, the dinner party becomes more and more chaotic and like a nightmare. 'Take care of yourself!' screams the Queen as Alice begins to grow bigger: 'Something's going to happen!' The candles suddenly shoot up to the ceiling, the bottles fly round the room with plates as wings, the leg of mutton sits in the Queen's chair, and the Queen herself falls grinning into the soup. As the soup ladle advances up the table towards her, Alice cries: 'I can't stand this any longer!' and pulls the table cloth, bringing everything crashing to the ground, at which the

Red Queen, who is a dominating, violent, and frightening person throughout the story, grows smaller, and is then seized and shaken by Alice until it is plain that she is in reality only a mischievous, friendly little kitten, after all. In the same way, at the end of *Alice in Wonderland*, the turbulent and hostile members of the law court are reduced by Alice to 'nothing but a pack of cards', and as these in their turn fly up and attack her, she wakes to find harmless, fluttering, dead leaves.

The inner life of phantasy never loses its meaning; the child who develops well grows to be less at the mercy of it, and more closely in contact with reality, but throughout life it underlies all his activities and is the core of his existence.

CHAPTER SEVEN

The Living-Through of Phantasies

EVERY child in his development must live through the phases discussed in earlier chapters, and, if that development is to be successful and complete, must experience deep feelings and find satisfying means of expressing his phantasies. Where a child is himself too deeply anxious or his environment too restrictive and disapproving, such expression is stifled or may be forced into undesirable channels, so that development is interfered with. The opposite was the case with Dinah, who up to the age of 3.4 (as at the time of writing) showed a happy, lively, and free personality based on the vivid expression of phantasies, and the full living-through of periods of anxiety and conflict. In what Dinah's history tells us of her parents' attitude to her and her problems, it illustrates the very great value to a child of understanding and real tolerance on the part of the adults, and while implying throughout an extremely good relationship between the three of them, shows clearly how, alongside this, the child's feelings of frustration, jealousy, hate and grief, phantasies of attack and punishment, and concepts of bad parents and a bad child inevitably exist. In this chapter, at the expense of repeating material already included, a detailed account of Dinah's early life is given, in order to trace her development as clearly as possible.

Dinah was the much-welcomed first child. During her first three years the family life was characterized, from a material point of view, by recurrent lack of money and by frequent moves

139

due to the parents' inability to get a settled home of their own, which were inevitably accompanied by anxiety and unrest. In general, however, Dinah seems to have led a secure life in an easy-going atmosphere, with a father who was devoted to her and openly admired her, and an unusually adaptable and understanding mother who could view her attachment to her father as something positive, and could tolerate her hostility to her, as well as accepting demonstrations of the very real affection she had for her.

During the first fortnight of Dinah's life, when she and her mother were in hospital, they were together only at feeding times. From the beginning she had a voracious appetite and would suck passionately, gulping down so much milk that she often vomited, and continuing to suck until the breast was emptied. At first she would scream with rage whenever her sucking was interrupted, even while being transferred from one breast to the other, and if kept waiting for her food for a minute or two would work herself up into an unusually intense state of anger; from the age of two months, however, she would stop crying when she saw her mother approaching, and smile and wave her arms in anticipation, and would then be more able to wait to be fed while preparations were made. In general, when unpleasant things happened, as for instance when defaecation was painful or she was fretting over a mosquito bite, Dinah could be comforted by being given the breast, but it was noticed at about ten weeks that if she had been very hungry and crying angrily, she would be in a state of tension and unable to feed at first; instead, she would turn from the breast and suck her own hands, or would turn her head round and round so that the nipple revolved in her mouth, clenching her fists, drumming her feet, and taking very shallow breaths, until at last she took a great gulp and began to suck.

At three and a half months the milk supply began to decrease, and there was not enough at the six o'clock feed. Dinah would continue to suck at the empty breast, and would protest when it was taken from her. She angrily refused the supplementary bottle, persisting in this for a fortnight, after which she accepted it. During the next three months, breast feeds were gradually decreased without resistance, until at six and a half months she was entirely on the bottle. The first solids were offered at four and a half months; Dinah sucked cheese off rusks with relish, and when later cereals and vegetables were introduced, they were accepted after one or two rejections, and subsequently much enjoyed. As already described on page 65, the first teeth did not appear until eight and a half months, when Dinah began spontaneously to turn from sucking to chewing, so that weaning from the bottle was carried out during the next month with particular ease; by nine and a half months, when she had two more teeth, she was preferring to twang the teat with her finger rather than suck it, and demanding rusks to chew at all times of the day. The need to suck was confined to the night-time ritual of the 'eating coat', which persisted until about two years: from the age of two months, Dinah had sucked something woolly before she fell asleep, first the blanket, and later a special knitted glove, vest, or coat, without which she could not settle down for the night.

For the first three months after weaning, Dinah ate enormous meals and drank large quantities of milk and orange juice. This was followed by a six-months period when she went off her food, which coincided both with the experience of pain in cutting more teeth, and with a stay in the country where she was very much disturbed by her father's frequent absences from home. Apart from this one period, and times when she completely rejected vegetables, her feeding was satisfactory, with great enjoyment of milk, eggs, and cheese, and normal likes and dislikes which were permitted without any forcing. Throughout, eating was a source of pleasure, and she had a positive relationship with her food, which, as we have already seen (p. 54), included the wish to ensure that the food she ate enjoyed being inside her.

During the first few months, the act of defaecation often appeared to be painful to Dinah, although her motions were quite loose; by four months, however, there were times when it obviously gave her pleasure, as for example on the occasion, already described after the insertion of a suppository. Between the ages of eleven months and one year she occasionally smeared her faeces, doing so quietly while she was in her play-pen and evidently enjoying it. When she was about a year, her mother began now and again to introduce the pot, but did not insist when each time it was refused. At 1.1 Dinah would sometimes lift her skirt with a slightly guilty air after wetting on the floor, and on seeing a puddle would exclaim: 'Oh God, wee-wee!'—even if, as on one occasion, it was only some spilt beer! When she was 1.3 and was going through an extremely positive and affectionate phase in regard to her mother, she would sit on the pot willingly, with an air of great pride and satisfaction, and would listen to the tinkle of urine with delight, chuckling. She would gaze at her mother with a loving smile when urinating or defaecating, and on some occasions clung to her and passionately pressed her face against hers. During this period she was sometimes reluctant to get off the pot, and liked to inspect and touch its contents, although she would not stay on it at all if left alone. This phase of using the pot was brief, and by 1.4 Dinah was vigorously refusing it again during a generally difficult period when she was cutting her teeth. On one occasion, when made to stay on it for ten minutes as an experiment, she threw the toys she had been given across the room, screaming with fury, and when allowed to get up looked at her mother with intense dislike, and saying 'bye bye' walked out, slamming the door behind her. A month later she cried unhappily when dirty, and began from time to time to ask for the pot herself, gradually becoming, in general, clean and dry without outside pressure. At the same time she showed pleasure and pride in being clean and tidy in many different ways. Dinah did not at any age show much anxiety over excretion, probably partly owing to her parents' calm and undemanding attitude towards it, but appeared to regard it as an enjoyable activity and topic for discussion; there were many lively comments, as for instance at 3.0: 'I want to be excused—do you know what that means? It means that my bottom's full up with wee-wee!' while a continual chant on the lavatory of 'I've done a wee-wee, I've done a big job!' was followed by the mock reprimand to herself: 'It's nothing to shout about really!'

This gay and placid attitude to life was a characteristic of Dinah's early general development, side by side with vigour, determination, and passion, such as has already been seen in the feeding situation. For instance, in her efforts to sit up and later to stand and walk, she would persist until crying with fatigue, relaxing into contentment only when at last the activity was successfully established. In the same way, besides long spells of happy babbling during the first year, there were at times intense efforts to attract the attention of strangers by means of vocalization, with bursts of anger on failure to do so. By 1.1 free walking had been achieved and Dinah was talking continuously, using twelve recognizable words together with her own jargon. During the next few months, her enthusiasm for experimental physical activity gradually gave place to an increasing delight in manipulative and social play; for instance, there was a great deal of housework, in imitation of the mother, and the beginning of doll play. By 2.0 she was playing mainly with dolls and toy animals, and was very much interested in pictures, particularly those of animals, which she would kiss and try to feed with chocolate, and comment on: 'Poor doggie din-din all gone'; 'Bow-wow jumping'; 'Dear tiny cat'. She loved to hear her mother say nursery rhymes, and would ask repeatedly for 'more torly-torly; Mummy read book'. She now had a vocabulary of over 600 words, began to refer to herself as 'I' instead of 'Dinah', to hold long monologues when playing, and to put more complex ideas into words, as for instance: 'Must go downstairs see Daddy', and 'That no good, throw it away.'

At all times she had a capacity for great enjoyment of life, and was generally in very good spirits, showing a keen sense of humour, as, for example, when she said (at 2.8): 'I went for a walk in a field and met some blue rain, and I asked that blue rain if it would like to come for a walk, and it said: "No, I wouldn't, because I'm only a *thing*!"' (laughing), and 'Flies can't ride on buses, because they've got no bottoms to sit on the seats!' She entered into all her activities with zest, and showed resourcefulness and fertility of imagination in her play; she could make use of almost anything that came to hand: a string of onions was put to bed with a hot-water bottle; a cheese grater was made a pet of, called a baby tiger, and kept in a saucepan in the larder; the bath-plug was used as a telephone for ringing up the water, while when standing up in the bath she would have her 'water socks' on. She showed much interest in such discoveries as that empty mugs floated while full ones sank, that the hot pipe led to the hot tap, that round things had oval shadows, and that coloured soap gave a white lather, and made many thoughtful comments and comparisons as, for example: (at 2.4) 'When I throw coal on the fire, it burns, and that's a very funny thing really. I don't know how that is'; (at 2.8) 'When it's a rainy day the sun hides in case he gets his hair wet'; (at 2.10 after watching an engine getting up steam) 'It's very like a kettle really'; and (at 3.0) 'On Thursday afternoon the shops are all Sundayed.' In order to bring out the various trends in Dinah's development, it has been necessary to extract material from the mother's very full day-to-day records of her and to group it, with the result that the picture of her as a whole child may be distorted if its context is forgotten. It is against such a background of happy, busy play that the phantasies and conflicts described in this chapter stand. Common to all children, they were expressed in Dinah's case with unusual vividness and force; at all times, however, even when anxiety was at its height, she gave evidence of a friendly, happy, serene, and basically undisturbed personality.

As already described, Dinah's earliest relationship with her mother centred in passionate and greedy feeding, involving intense enjoyment of sucking and a very positive acceptance of the good food her mother offered her. Appreciation of the mother as the giver of good things was shown at two months, when she would stop crying and smile at her approach; loving feelings, together with a generous wish to give her back something good, were apparent at ten months, when she repeatedly interrupted the feeding of herself to put food into her mother's mouth, and, as already described, at 1.3 when she clung affectionately and smilingly to her while urinating and defaecating. When Dinah was able to talk, there were many verbal expressions of admiration and love for her. For instance, at 3.2 she remarked: 'I kiss you on the ear because you're such a dear Mummy.' On being asked: 'What makes me such a dear?' she replied: 'Oh, just by being my Mummy'; while at times she addressed her as: 'dear Mummy', 'boo'ful Mummy', and 'darling Mummy buttons'—'buttons' being her name for nipples. From the first, 'Mum-mum' seemed to mean: 'I need something'; as a background the mother stood for something constant and inevitable, a source of security; her pronouncements were always held by Dinah to be right, without question, and would be repeated frequently to other people. When Dinah asked her father a question, she would often verify his reply by consulting her mother, and if their statements did not entirely coincide would say indignantly: 'My Mummy doesn't say that!' Moreover, while she talked about 'Daddy', it was generally 'my Mummy'.

Apart from the appreciation of the mother as the giver of good and necessary things, another aspect of the feeding relationship was the insistent demand that suckling should continue as long as Dinah wished, with intolerance of interruptions, and suspicious distrust of the breast that had not been under her control and there when she wanted it, as expressed in her inability to start feeding at once after a period of angry waiting. This wish to possess and control the mother was shown in attempts at all ages to dominate her activities: for instance, at times the mother was not allowed to whistle, sing, or cross her legs, or to say certain nursery rhymes which, Dinah said, were hers. She would sometimes do her best to prevent her mother from reading and would also try to stop her talking, putting her hand over her mouth and herself shouting and singing loudly to silence her, while she liked to order her activities, trying to insist, for instance, that the washing-up should be done at a particular time. At the same time, there was frequent resistance of what Dinah felt to be her mother's attempts to control and interfere with *her* activities. She would insist on doing the housework herself, refusing to let her mother have the broom or dustpan if she was using it, looking up furiously when her mother came to the door while she was washing the bathroom floor at 1.5, and saying at 2.3, when her washing-up was interrupted: 'You can go away in an aeroplane if you like.' At times she would attack her without apparent provocation, sometimes in earnest but usually in play, pulling her hair, pinching her, making movements as if to gouge out her eyes, slapping her face, and biting her arms, while when prevented from biting she would often bang her own head in frustration.

At two and a half months one way of coping with the situation of the unsatisfying, deserting breast and with her own overpowering anger towards it was, as we have seen, to turn away from it and suck her own hands, or to play with the nipple in her mouth but refuse to suck. At three and a half months, during the fortnight the six o'clock feed failed and she was fighting to continue sucking the empty breast and furiously refusing the bottle, Dinah began on occasions to turn her face away from her mother, when in her father's arms, and refuse to smile at her, although she would continue to beam at him. It seems as if in her anger with her mother over the frustrations of feeding she turned from her to the father, perhaps with the feeling that she could gain from him the good thing her mother refused her. Throughout Dinah's early years there were times, such as these, when she would reject her mother in favour of her father; for instance, at 1.1 she would sit on her father's knee and say to her mother with an air of finality: 'Bye bye'. These particular attitudes to the parents were reflected in her reactions to strangers: up to about 1.8 she would turn away from strange women, but would accost strange men with the words 'Man, man', and run up to them smiling, while she would follow men visitors about, and liked them to do things for her, in place of her mother.

Dinah's father was looked on by her as a source of excitement and pleasure, an attitude which was obviously enhanced by the fact that he was, himself, a stimulating and exciting person who flattered and made much of her. From the age of a few months she would go to sleep in his arms when nothing could be found to soothe her, and as soon as she could speak, the word 'Dada' was used to denote all pleasant experiences, while at a later date, when she used it to refer to him, she would say it in a particularly loving tone of voice. From the time Dinah was about a year old, the family lived in the country for some months, and the father had to be away during the week. During his absences Dinah would mourn for him, calling continually for 'Dada'. She would hunt through newspapers for pictures of 'Dada', and having once spoken to him on the telephone demanded passionately to do so again and again. Sometimes she would suddenly gaze at his chair with a rapt expression, and a beaming smile would come over her face, but soon fade, as if for a moment she had seen him there; while on one occasion she suddenly said: 'Dada!' and, smiling with delight, hurried upstairs to his bedroom and peeped excitedly round the door as if expecting to find him there, but on seeing his bed empty burst into tears. She would keep scraps of her dinner for him, and loved to play at buying things for him to eat, and at a later date, when she had to go to bed before he had come home from work in the evening, would wail: 'Daddy *still* in motor-car; I want little tiny talka Daddy!' At 1.1 she became passionately attached to a toy dog at the times when her father was away: she would say: 'Bow-wow!' in an ecstatic voice, smiling broadly and clasping it to her chest, kissing its head and pressing her face to it, while tending to ignore it on his return. Once, when Dinah was 1.5, the father had to go away again after a fortnight's holiday at home. When they arrived at the station, Dinah cried in despair: 'Daddy gone!' and when he eventually got on to the train, burst into tears. After the train had departed, she searched for him hopefully among the people leaving the station. Her mother took her on to the beach, where she played in a solitary and preoccupied way, wandering quite a long way away and making little contact. Throughout the rest of the day she played quietly on her own, and when her mother said goodnight to her at bedtime, she pushed her hand aside and silently turned her head away. A week or two later she was her usual active and jolly self, but the mother sensed an underlying note of sadness.

Some months later this sadness was seen again, but in relation to her mother. At this time Dinah (1.5) was going through a phase of hostility towards her, with redoubled affection for her father. She would get into bed with him and sometimes refuse to let her mother in, sitting beside him, kissing him and rubbing noses, and calling him 'dear Daddy'. When her mother asked: 'Am I dear Mummy?' she laughed and said: 'No—Mummy naughty!'

She much enjoyed displaying herself to her father, saying: 'Pretty dress, look, pretty coat; pretty Dinah!' There were other moments when she would gaze at her mother with a puzzled, yearning, unhappy expression. Several times she put mud or grass on her mother's clothes and then vigorously wiped it off, saying: 'Mummy dirty-clean', and one night in bed repeated several times: 'Dinah dirty.' When her mother asked what was dirty, she replied: 'Dirty feet', and showed them to her; they were quite clean, but earlier in the day she had been worried by some mud she had noticed between her mother's toes when they were sunbathing. On another occasion when her mother had taken something away from her, Dinah immediately hit the dog which was standing nearby, then kissed it, saying sadly: 'Poor bow-wow!' Subsequent material points to how very real was Dinah's grief over a mother whom she felt to be attacked and injured, and how very heartfelt was her wish to restore her. Such moments of depression and preoccupation had been noted by the mother as early as approximately three to five months, when Dinah would lie quite still in her pram as her mother wheeled her along, gazing sadly up at the sky, instead of smiling and waving as usual. Also at 1.4, during a period when she was clinging to her and unable to be happy when she was out of sight, she woke one night sobbing: 'All gone is Mum-mum!' and when picked up and comforted, said: 'Bad Mum-mum!' Moreover, there were times when she turned back to her mother from her father, wanting her in preference to him, and behaving most lovingly towards her.

As time went on, many phantasies relating to the parents became manifest. Dinah's father and mother did not prohibit her from going into the bathroom when they were bathing, and she much enjoyed 'washing' them. She made no comments on their bodies nor compared them with her own until, when she was 1.10, the family went to live with some friends who had a little boy, Harold, of the same age. After her first bath with Harold, she pulled down her dolls' knickers to inspect their genital areas, and smiled in a satisfied way, and two days later she commented on her father's 'tail' in the bath. From this time, Dinah showed in many vivid ways her feeling that she lacked a penis. She began to be concerned over her own genitals, complaining that her 'bottom' hurt and asking to have cream put on it. She also often examined her dolls, commenting: 'Got no tailies', and one day said the same of her teddy bear, having previously discovered that he was coming unstitched at the groin. At other times she remarked: 'Water got no hands'; 'Teddy got no hands'; 'Dolly got no teeth—oh, Mummy going to buy some for dolly!'; 'Dolly got no nose'; 'Elephant got no red mouth,' and she liked to point out familiar objects and say what they were *not*, for example: 'That's *not* a doggie, that's a pussy-cat really.' When out she would keep up a ceaseless chant about things she saw in the shops, saying: 'Can't have that dolly—that's Harold's', 'Can't have that train—that's Harold's'—a feeling that was reinforced by the fact that Harold was extremely possessive over his toys, and there were many things of his which Dinah could not have, in reality. There was also much crying over bumps and tumbles, and she seemed abnormally sensitive to physical injury. She was very anxious to 'wee-wee' standing up, envying her cousin Jim (a few months older), who called it 'doing tinks', and made many experiments, which resulted in constant puddles on the floor in which she trampled. On one occasion she asked her father to 'wee-wee' in her pot while she used Jim's, and another time said she wanted to 'wee-wee standing up in Daddy's pot' (i.e. the lavatory).

Certain things seemed to suggest that Dinah held her mother responsible for her deprivation. For instance, on the day on which she first commented on her father's 'tail', she suddenly grabbed a knife which her mother was using, and in doing so cut herself, at which she walked silently to a chair on the other side of the room and sat down with an air of great resentment, eventually saying: 'Go away, horrid Mummy!' On several occasions she accused her mother of biting her or hurting her finger, and while in general the friendly relationship between the two of them was maintained, there were times when she seemed to regard her mother's daily care of her as an attack or potential danger, running to her father for protection. One day, having been very much upset when her mother washed her hair, Dinah said through her sobs: 'I like that hairwash. Mummy not a horrid girl, Mummy a good girl really.' Here she seemed to be trying in vain to fight against her conviction that her mother was cruelly attacking her. A week or two later, after having again been much distressed at having her hair washed, she complained in bed that her toes were too short. She said: 'Harold's a boy; Celia's a girl; David bite!' and burst into tears. She then asked for 'Daddy's baby dolly', one of a pair of miniature dolls, the other of which she said belonged to her mother. On another occasion she woke in the night crying: 'Doggy hurta foot.' During this whole period she was cutting her back teeth, and it seems likely that the very real pain she experienced was woven into her phantasies of being attacked and injured. At this time, as described in Chapter I, she showed marked fear of going down the waste-pipe in the bath, of a new charwoman, and of the salvage woman who collected the newspapers, saying: 'Little lady take away Mummy papers', and that she 'wanted to take away Dinah'. As already suggested, it seems possible that Dinah's fear of being taken away by the salvage woman (and perhaps too by the waste-pipe when her mother pulled the plug) arose because she felt herself to be the 'little lady' who took away Mummy's papers, since it was she who proudly carried her father's newspaper up to him in bed each morning—that is, she took away her mother's privilege in relation to the father.

This points to the fact that alongside Dinah's sense of having been attacked and deprived by her mother, there was a feeling that the mother herself was injured. One day she remarked, on inspecting the washing: 'Mummy's knick-knicks broken; must buy another one in a shop'—although they were really intact. On another occasion an argument between them was followed by the mother's jamming her finger in the door, over which Dinah showed curiosity but apparent lack of concern, discussing with interest the possibility of the nail falling off. On the other hand, when they went out for a walk she vehemently refused to hold the damaged hand, almost as if afraid of it, and remarked later: 'Mummy hurta fingy. Dinah cutta fingy'; and then 'Dolly hurta head. Make all better', demanding bandages for it, insisting that they were 'clean', and patting it lovingly. Here clearly the feelings of pity and wish to heal expressed to the doll really related to the mother. In general, Dinah showed great solicitude for her dolls at this time, often saying they were hurt, and applying cotton wool and cold cream most tenderly, saying: 'All better now'; 'Never mind, dear dolly'; 'Poor dolly crying: I want to make dolly happy.' Sometimes she would throw one on the floor, and then immediately pick it up and comfort it lovingly, while at about this time she also started to tear her books, and was full of remorse about the damage she had done to a favourite one, saying: 'I torn that little tiny hole in the book. Naughty Dinah! Daddy take it away. Poor little Mother Goose book. Naughty book!' On another occasion, when she very much wanted to play with a doll belonging to an older child and was told that she could not, she buried her head in her mother's shoulder in silent grief, spontaneously giving the explanation that she might break it. In all these situations there is evidence of feelings of guilt and grief over damage done to objects which, in each case seemed to represent the mother.

It was perhaps this guilt about her attacks on the mother that lay behind Dinah's evident anxiety that she would be deserted by her: she would cling to her, and follow her round the house, as if afraid to let her out of her sight, and when playing in the garden would on occasions suddenly run in crying; on finding her mother there her face would break into smiles, and she would exclaim with relief: 'Oh, I thought you'd gone away in an aeroplane!' Any baby she saw crying was said to have 'lost his mummy', and she herself would frequently cry at night, and work herself up into a state of distress if her mother did not come to her. Also, she would try to wheedle her mother to stay with her instead of doing the household jobs: 'Mummy don't want to go away now really. Mummy want to come in the garden now.'

Without stimulus from her parents Dinah began to show, in general, a consciousness of 'naughtiness'. For several days she discussed things one 'mustn't touch', as for example gas taps. She said one must not touch a motor-car 'because it's got something in it—a man', and when pulling the wheels off a toy car; said she must not touch the 'Mummy wheel', but gave her father the 'Daddy wheel'. On several occasions she remarked laughingly: 'Shouldn't do that really', although what she was doing was permitted, and one night after her bath was found standing at the top of the stairs saying to herself: 'No!—not to go downstairs. No!' At this time she began kindly but firmly to discipline her dolls, particularly at their bedtime, telling them not to go downstairs, not to cry, not to touch the gas taps, etc. It is perhaps significant that she was at this time masturbating more than usual. Once when lying on the bed she touched her genitals and shouted with delighted laughter, saying 'Bottom!'; another time, when her mother was putting cream on, she gleefully called for 'more cream on bottom'; some weeks later, while in the bath, she said: 'I like my bottom; I want my bottom; Mummy, let I play with my bottom'; while on another occasion she pushed Coco, the toy monkey, up her knickers and closed her legs tightly, looking amused. She was also at this time wanting to see both her parents' genitals, and while sitting on her pot one day and touching hers, was heard to murmur 'Mummy lady' over and over again. On these occasions she did not appear at all guilty or embarrassed by the presence of her mother, who showed no disapproval. On the other hand, when one day she was masturbating on her pot and her mother said: 'Don't do that', in quite a mild tone of voice, she instantly took her hand away, saying: 'No', as if she felt she was doing something wrong. It seems possible that some of Dinah's insistence on what she should not touch and should not do might have had at its root a guilt about masturbatory activities and the phantasies accompanying them.

She showed anxiety about stories that were 'rough', and on one occasion when her mother broke a cup, insisted that she herself had done it. She was worried by a picture of a monkey stealing cherries from a woman's hat, wanting to turn over the page 'to see some good people', and saying: 'The monkey was naughty, when he was good he put them back.' When looking at a symbolic picture on a magazine cover which showed a large head of a man, a small man, and a clenched fist, she related how the tiny man was running away because he had taken the big man's pencil, which the big man wanted back, although there was, in fact, no sign of a pencil in the picture. The hand, she said, was a lady's hand with chocolates in it; the lady wanted to take the pencil away from the tiny man and give it back to the big man.

It seems possible that this story, in which the little man takes the pencil from the big man, expressed Dinah's wish to obtain a penis from her father, while the fact that it is the lady who wants him to give it back might suggest that Dinah felt that to possess it would be to rob her mother. This wish for something from the father had been shown earlier when, distressed because her toes were too short, she cried for 'Daddy's baby dolly', and in her statement after a hairwashing episode, on remembering that her father had a moustache, that she had one too—'a little one, but nobody else'. This may throw light on the reason why Dinah felt that her mother was injured ('Mummy's knick-knicks broken') and therefore intent on attacking and injuring her back. The wish to deprive her mother in relation to her father was also shown directly. At this time, she would demand that she slept in her parents' room, saying: 'This is *my* room. This is *my* beddy.' She would also wake in the night and wail repeatedly: 'I want to go bye-bye Daddy now!' In the morning she liked to get into bed beside her father, and on more than one occasion remarked with evident pleasure: 'Daddy bottom, Daddy taily!' When her mother came back into the room, however, she would spontaneously get out of bed, as if she felt she had displaced her.

When these phantasies seemed to be in full sway, Dinah (1.11) became acutely afraid of motor-cars, which up to this time had always been associated with her father: she would clutch her mother's hand in the street, saying: 'Car coming!' and showed alarm at the noise of air coming out of motor tyres. She also showed great terror of Harold, and would whine and cling to her mother, making no attempt to retaliate when he took her toys or refused to let her share his. Although Harold was, in fact, aggressive, her extreme reaction to him seemed out of proportion to the reality situation: she would often turn pale, saying: 'Harold's coming!' and would rush to climb on to her mother's knee and stay there for half an hour at a time, saying anxiously: 'Come right upa Mummy—*no* down!' It seems possible that Harold represented, in part, her 'naughty' self—the monkey who had stolen the cherries, and the little man who had stolen the big man's pencil—that is, the child with the penis. At the same time, in so far as 'Harold coming' was equated with 'Car coming', and she envied him his penis, it is likely that he also stood for a revengeful father. At this point it seems as if the frightening and retaliatory aspects of the father were split off, and were only seen in terms of Harold and motor-cars, while the father himself remained an idealized figure, entirely devoted to her. On the other hand, certain things she said seemed to suggest that she felt that he, too, was injured; for example: 'Poor Daddy can't come home now', and (also while he was away): 'Daddy's crying. I want to make Daddy happy. Daddy's a good man.'

During this period Dinah was very much enjoying urinating standing up every day in the bath, after which she would trample in the water in the same way in which she had gleefully and triumphantly trampled in puddles of urine. She also instituted a particular game at bathtime: on the first day she pinched her chest and then poured water over it to 'make it all better', stating: 'Harold pinched me this morning' (which was untrue); the next day when her mother was having a bath she commented on her 'baby buttons' (nipples), and poured water over them, saying: 'Baby buttons like that'; while at night-time, when having her own bath, she again poured water over her chest, and said that her father had pinched her. On the third night she filled a basin with water, saying: 'Huge Daddy water', and poured it over herself, and then put a little water in it and repeated the process, saying: 'Little tiny Mummy water.' This was done several times, mostly with full 'Daddy' basins of water, and was much enjoyed. Dinah commented on how dirty the water was, and also said: 'I'm a bow-bow.' Another day, when her mother got her up from rest, Dinah angrily accused her of smacking her for having wet her bed, although in fact her mother had not reprimanded her in any way. She then said: 'Dear Mummy!' and tried to open her mother's dress, saying: 'Where are Mummy's buttons?' and 'Kiss Mummy's chest better.' These attempts at reparation indicate that Dinah unconsciously equated her current aggression towards her mother with her infantile attacks on the breast, pinching and bed-wetting perhaps representing her original angry biting and urinating. It seems that because the first turning to the father at the age of three months had been an angry rejection of the frustrating breast, in her present turning to him it was the breast—the original object of her attacks—which was felt to be injured. She tried to heal it not only by kissing it, but by returning to it the father she had stolen in giving it 'huge Daddy waters', that is, unlimited quantities of good, soothing, masculine urine, represented by the 'dirty' bath-water into which as a 'bow-wow' she had urinated in a standing position. From this one might infer that to Dinah part of the value in general of having a penis was to be able to produce magic urine with which to heal the injured mother— that is, herself to become the father.

This attempt to identify with the father was expressed in many other ways in Dinah's play: she often pretended to be Daddy, to shave, and to drive away in a bus, and had a special game called 'playing my office'. At the beginning of this period she was able, too, to identify with and thus from one point of view openly to rival her mother, while at the same time she was extremely affectionate and full of admiration for her. On one occasion when she was stroking her mother's hair and saying 'Boo'ful Mummy', she started stroking her own, saying: 'Dinah boo'ful hair!' She would stand admiring herself in front of the glass, and would ask for bracelets or a bow in her hair, and say she wanted to be pretty like her mother, once remarking: 'I'm *Miss* Dinah really.' She loved to do housework and to cook, making shapes out of pastry to give to her father, and would often state: 'Mummy lady' and 'I'm a lady.' Soon after her second birthday, however, she started vehemently denying that she was a little girl or a lady, and insisted that she was a baby: 'Mummy's a lady; Daddy's a man; I'm a little tiny baby.' She called herself 'baby Dinah', and wanted to be carried and to have things done for her, and to be given frequent drinks of milk. This reversion to infancy must have had many meanings for her; among other things, it was perhaps an attempt to find a solution to the problems of her aggressive wishes to take away the father's penis and to rival the mother, since a baby, as the alternative to a boy or girl, seemed in Dinah's mind at this time to have been sexless.

This phase continued for about two months, but towards the end of the period, while still murmuring when she was being cuddled by her mother that she was 'Mummy's little tiny baby', she began again to assume other roles, fluctuating from one to the other. There were more attempts to 'wee-wee standing-up', and the statement: 'I'm a boy; I'm Jim.' At the same time Dinah showed proud maternal feelings for her doll, and would continually feed it, wash it, and put it to bed, talking to it and handling it with the greatest tenderness. Once she said: 'Daddy likes my baby very much', and later: 'This is my baby really; not Mummy's baby, not Daddy's baby—no, Dinah's baby'; while there were times when she decided to call the doll Dinah instead of Mary, saying: 'This is another little baby called Dinah', as if, now able to feel more grown-up, she was investing the doll with the baby part of herself. One evening she said: 'I'm a boy', but the next night, for the first time for a long time: 'I'm a little girlie.' This statement she repeated several times during the next few days, and once remarked, putting on her mother's stockings: 'I'm a lady now', and another time: 'Baby can have my little shoes; I have my mummy's shoes.' She would also declare that she was a 'big grown-up girl', and would once again stand in front of the glass, admiring herself and saying: 'I'm pretty.' Gradually she ceased to be 'a little tiny baby' altogether; instead, her mother and father were sometimes babies and had to be put to bed by her, while she was able to look back on the time when she herself was a baby, replying—when asked: 'Was it nice?'—'Yes, it was comfy.'

At the same time she was working out the physical differences between the sexes. One day she announced that she had 'a little taily' underneath her 'bottom', and that her mother had one too, but on another occasion, having stated that she was a boy, she immediately contradicted herself, saying: 'Not a boy really: a 'tend boy.' Three weeks later, inspecting her genitals while sitting on the pot, she remarked with a humorous expression: 'I got no taily', and at another time: 'Mummy got no taily. Daddy got one, and Jim, too.' She would also frequently murmur 'Sit down' or 'girlie' to herself while urinating, although still very much enjoying the game of 'doing tinks' in the bath. These problems were also worked out with her dolls. She commented affectionately on 'Teddy's little woolly bottom', and he was made to sit on the pot 'and not do tinks'. She said: 'Teddy's got his little bottom to do wee-wee; no, not to stand up—to wee-wee sitting down', and 'Sometimes Teddy's a naughty boy, and sometimes Teddy's a good boy.' She also said: 'Sometimes dolly can do tinks'; 'Baby girl can't do tinks, has to sit on pot'; and 'Horsie can't do wee-wee at all 'cos he's got no bottom.' She also became able to admire boys in a more positive way: for instance, one day she watched intently while her cousin Jim urinated, and then flung her arms round him, saying lovingly: 'Oh, Jim, Jim, I'm trying to pick you up.' Together with Dinah's increasing ability to acknowledge that she was a girl and could only pretend to be a boy came an acceptance of the differences between herself and her mother. She compared 'Mummy's huge 'normous tummy' with her own little one, and stated: 'Baby doll has weeny bottom; Dinah has little bottom; Mummy has huge 'normous bottom'; and: 'When I'm a mummy I shall have hair on my bottom.'

At the time that Dinah showed this change in attitude to her mother, there appeared a new element of feeling towards her father. He was no longer only the over-idealized person, incapable of retaliation and all-loving in his attitude to her. She remarked: 'I don't like Daddy very much. He takes Dinah's things', and: 'I'll show Daddy my sweeties—no, he might take them away.' On another day, she said laughingly before going to play with her father: 'I'm a little bit frightened of Daddy', while she asserted that she was *not* frightened of ducks (having previously insisted that the big duck was a 'daddy duck, not a mummy duck'), and became interested in Miss Muffet's fear of a spider. A few days earlier she had shown some fear of a toy tortoise, saying: 'I like that tortoise a little bit, but not too much.' Later she related how the naughty tortoise had pinched and bitten her, and touched the chair where the dolls slept. A month later she climbed up to look at a picture of a naked man in a bathroom, and said: 'I don't like that tortoise. That man's a tortoise. I'm frightened of that tortoise-man'; while another day she said: 'I don't like mans really.'

Although still somewhat suspicious of interference with her activities on the mother's part, Dinah, showed at this time (approximately 2.3–2.6) a definite preference and much positive feeling for her. She said with admiration one day: 'You're so clever, Mummy: you can cook and sew and eat up your dinner and go to bed.' She began to defend her mother's rights and pre-rogatives, saying such things as: 'Naughty Mary doing Mummy's ironing', and: 'Daddy, *don't* play with Mummy's washing-up!' She also showed much evidence of the feeling of guilt towards her and wish to restore her which had appeared earlier, asserting that it was she who had bought her mother's new cup for her, and that she had scraped the mud off her mother's shoes and cleaned them for her, both of which were not so, while a favourite game was to make her mother pretend to cry by smacking and pinching her, and then pat her better tenderly, saying: 'Don't cry!' She also spent much time making dolls' beds, cooking dinners, cleaning and mending: 'I have to clean this 'cos it's got a little bit dirty', 'I have to mend that 'cos it's got broken'; and she liked to play at bandaging imaginary 'baddies' (sore places), saying: 'I'm mending me; I'm making me better.'

When Dinah was 2.6, the family had a chicken for lunch which had eggs in it, and explanations were given to her older cousins. Dinah herself did not seem interested at the time, but a few days later, at bedtime, she asked: 'Have you got eggs in your tummy like a chicken, Mummy?' Her mother replied 'No', feeling later that her answer had been terse and inadequate. During the course of the next week Dinah spent much time playing at being a baby bird; she asked: 'Where's the fire's mummy?' and when told: 'Fires don't have mummies; only people and animals have mummies', she said: 'And eggs?' This might suggest that she had not, in fact, accepted her mother's negative reply to her question about eggs inside her. As already commented on in Chapter V, one of Dinah's favourite games a month earlier had been to make 'secrets' in boxes, and to build brick houses enclosing a little dog, or 'little Mr. Brick'. Two months later, her favourite dolls were two very small ones called 'Grows' ('because she's so tiny') and 'Wonks Tonks', and they were not put to bed because, she said, they liked to sleep in her overcoat pocket with the flap down to keep them warm. Her mother was at this time three months pregnant, but Dinah had not, as yet, been told anything about it, although one cannot preclude the possibility that she had heard talk about it.

One day she spontaneously remarked: 'Mans can't have babies.' Later she said: 'What does Jim have a taily for?' Her mother replied: 'So as to be a daddy when he grows up', and Dinah said: 'Jim has a tiny weeny taily, and when he grows up he will have a huge enormous taily like his daddy Peter and my daddy Ben, and then everybody will have two daddies.' One day, while examining herself in the bath, the following conversation took place:

Dinah: 'Little boys have got tailies there, but I haven't. What have I got?'

Mother: 'A little hole.'

Dinah: 'And what does go into that hole?'

Mother: 'Nothing just now.'

Another day, also examining her genitals:

Dinah: 'What's that called?'

Mother: 'It's a little hole.'

Dinah: 'Who lives in that hole?'

Mother: 'Nobody.'

Dinah: 'That's a pretend house and pretend people live in it. What's it called? What does Daddy call it?'

Mother: 'What would you like to call it?'

Dinah: 'Noot, because only pretend people live in it.'

Mother: 'What sort of people?'

Dinah: 'Pretend *baby* people. Is it a taily?'

Mother: 'No.'

Dinah: 'What does Daddy have a taily for?'

Mother: 'All daddies have tailies.'

In these conversations Dinah clearly showed that she very well knew the functions of the penis and vagina, although she had never been told. A week later she examined her genitals again, sitting on the bed, and said, pointing to her clitoris: 'That's a little taily, and the wee-wee lives in there. Wee-wee and big-job go bye-bye in there.' Her mother said: 'The big-job comes out of another hole at the back.' Dinah investigated and asked the name of the anus, and then returned to her examination of the vulva saying: 'That's a hole where the wee-wee comes out, and that's another hole' (pointing to the vagina). She continued to touch it, repeating: 'It's called tilly-pilly-o-pint', and when asked why, she replied: 'Because that's its name.' From this time, girls were described as having 'pillies' instead of 'no tailies'.

During this period Dinah showed two contrasting attitudes to her mother, for at the same time as protesting that she was not wanting to take her place, she displayed a strong sense of rivalry and wish to get rid of her. For example, when one day her father twisted a piece of silver paper into a ring for her, she took it off

instantly, saying: 'I don't have a ring because I'm not a mummy';
and when she was playing with a doll which was 'tiny weeny
only just begun to be born', and her mother asked: 'Are you that
baby's mummy?' she replied: 'No, I'm not a mummy really,
I'm a little girl. You're the baby's mummy and I'm the pretend
mummy.' On the other hand, she frequently told her mother she
did not want her any more, saying, for instance: 'You go away
in an aeroplane and I will marry Daddy'; and on one occasion,
after having asked the meaning of 'husband', 'wife', and 'married',
she stated: 'I'm Daddy's wife, and we're married.'

At this point, perhaps because the conflicts over her parents
were too great, Dinah turned away from both of them.
She reacted with much aggression to any frustration, and evidently expected retaliation from them, since she suddenly remarked one day: 'You mustn't break me up, because I'd be all
gone. If you break me up, Mummy and Daddy will live at 61
all by themselves.' Meanwhile she turned with great affection to
Miss P., another adult living in the house, and could hardly be
persuaded to leave her. When one day her mother laughingly
asked: 'Have you finished with me?' she replied: 'Not quite.'
One night at bedtime she said to her mother: 'You're my proper
mummy; Miss P. is my other mummy', and then (as already
quoted) added: 'Miss P. is my best mummy. She's my good
mummy, and you're my naughty mummy.'

Dinah was 2.9 when her mother (then four months pregnant)
said to her: 'Would you like us to make a real baby?' Dinah
said: 'Yes, a baby sister. What would you make it from?' The
mother replied: 'It would grow in my tummy', and Dinah
seemed delighted with the idea. Later the following conversation
took place:

Dinah: 'I don't like before I was born. Where did I live before
I was born? I don't know.'

Mother: 'In my tummy.'

Dinah: 'And did you eat me up?'

Mother: 'No.'

Dinah: 'And what did I eat?'

Mother: 'Some of my food, because you were in my tummy.'

Dinah seemed pleased with this explanation, and wanted to be cuddled. Later, she tried to get inside her mother's dress, saying: 'I want to get into your tummy and have a drink of milk from your buttons', and also made attempts to do the same with her father. She wanted to know about time and death, and asked endless questions about babies and their habits, and seemed especially interested to hear of their incompetence. She also wanted to know what her mother did when she was a little girl, but was concerned to think that then she herself had no mummy, saying with consternation: 'Before you was born, where was me?'

She made up many stories about her dolls' origins, saying that Libberbel used to be a man and shave, and that she used to live in Africa and have a black face and red hair. All her dolls were once angels with brown dresses and brown faces, she said, and then they took off their wings and grew little, at which she put them in a pram and looked after them. Another time, the mother mentioned a time before Dinah was born.

Dinah (with marked displeasure): 'I don't like to be born. Little girls *don't* be born.'

Mother: 'Are little boys born?'

Dinah: 'Yes, but little girls don't be born because it's a little bit naughty. It would make me all black on my tummy.'

These references to black and brown might suggest that Dinah was at this time equating babies with faeces, and that she believed birth to occur by way of the anus, as undoubtedly was the case some months later when she insisted that *her* baby was going to come out of her 'back pilly' (already quoted, p. 77).

She began to enjoy making plasticine babies, and would also wrap dolls up in towels, saying that they were eggs and sitting on them to hatch them out. One day she remarked: 'Libberbel has two mummies called Dinah and Elisabeth, but only one daddy' (Elisabeth being her mother's name), while on another day she announced that she was Libberbel's mummy, and that her mother was the daddy—'So Libberbel has two daddies and only one mummy.' She also related how, when she was a big lady, Libberbel grew in her tummy; when she was big enough to come out, she tapped on it, made a little hole at the navel, and climbed out, carefully replacing it. Her mother explained which hole it was that babies came out of, and also denied the doll's birth, but said that Dinah would be able to have real babies when she grew up. Dinah emphatically rejected this, insisting that the doll did grow in her tummy. On one occasion Libberbel herself was said to be a mother, with a husband, Mr. Kingfinks, an engine-driver: 'They have two babies, a big girl and a little girl, but no boys because they don't want any boys. Libberbel baths the big girl in the bathroom, and Mr. Kingfinks washes the baby on his lap in the bedroom. Mr. Kingfinks has to wear a blouse like a lady, because the washing machine has broken all the buttons off his shirts. Then the mummy and daddy go away, and the little girls look after themselves, the big one holding the little one's hand.' Another time she remarked to her mother: 'When I'm a big lady Jim will be a big man, and then he can be my wife and help me shell peas. You will be a tiny baby then, and Jim can be your daddy'; while later she said: 'Teddy is now getting to be a very big boy and he will marry Libberbel soon, and Mary will marry Golliwog.'

In this material we see something of Dinah's struggle with her feelings of rivalry in relation both to the expected baby and to the mother herself. Sometimes her father was made into a second mother, so that the baby need not take her mother away from her; sometimes she and her mother shared the baby, while sometimes she was the 'mummy' while her mother was relegated to the position of a 'daddy' or a 'baby'. The intensity of her wish to get possession of the mother's baby was seen when, at the age of 3.0, having been frustrated by her, she asked her father to 'carve Mummy up and take the baby out of her tummy and give it to me'. She began to relate sadistic stories, as for instance one about the bad queen in *Snow White*, who had her eyes and tongue pulled out by a dwarf: 'Then she was cut up and cooked in the oven, and pierced all over with a sharp stone till she was full of holes and all worn out. Then she was thrown into the sea.' Another one concerned a man who shot a pirate's hat and legs off and shot his gun away: 'Then he cooked him in the oven and threw him into the sea for the fishes to eat up.' 'And', she added with great glee, 'what did that man do then, when the fishes had eaten him up and he was all gone?' She would playfully attack her parents, exclaiming: 'I'm going to kill you dead because I don't want you any more', and 'You're not to fight me because I'm very busy breaking you up.' There were times, too, when her aggression towards them broke through openly and earnestly; after biting her mother in the stomach, she said: 'I don't like Mummy any more because she upsets me', while she complained of her father that 'he doesn't look after me properly because he doesn't agree with me.'

At this time Dinah was asking innumerable questions about the olden days, the seasons, people in other countries, 'what makes wee-wee and big-jobs', 'why blood comes out of baddies', where the bath-water comes from, which animals are fierce, and why some people are naughty. She took special notice of anything cracked, broken, or shabby, asking: 'Who did it?' and was particularly interested in houses that were in a state of disrepair, and would gaze at those damaged by bombs, commenting on the broken windows and asking: 'Didn't the bomb like that house?' and stating that: 'All bombs are naughty' and: 'Libberbel killed all the bombs and threw them in the sea, so that they couldn't knock down any more houses.' She very much approved of builders and painters and asked many questions about their work, and in her play spent much time building houses with bricks. The following is an extract from a soliloquy carried on during brick-building play: 'This one must be in the corner of this one. It's got a chimney, and that's for the chimney-man to climb on. It has to have a very high step to climb up, and this is the bottom step for the little pretend chimney-man to climb up. These are the back steps—you see it has to have steps for climbing up on. This is a very high step, and this is where the smoke comes out. Now it's made, but nobody is allowed to go in until it's cleaned outside and inside.' She was also, at this time building large and compli-cated structures 'for babies to live in'. These interests occurred at a time when Dinah's family were living in London in a house which did not belong to them and which had only been lent for a very limited period, and as they had nowhere else to go, the whole matter was causing the parents some anxiety. Dinah would talk about an imaginary house in which the family were going to live: it had fresh white walls, two lavatories, and three refriger-ators, and she expressed a great longing for it. Apart from such reality influences, Dinah's interests in destroying and restoring buildings probably related to phantasies as to what she had done to her mother's body in her jealous efforts to take her baby from her, and expressed a wish to be able to rebuild her and make her whole again. Possibly she wanted to know about the olden days because she had a longing to get back to the time before the destruction took place, and also to the time when she herself was the baby.

Her guilt about the 'naughtiness' of her wishes to prevent her mother from having a baby, and at the same time her feel-ings of aggression towards the baby itself, were shown in the attacks she made on her dolls. For instance, she threw a favourite doll, Mary, on the floor, and kicked it so that its head broke, remarking with an air of satisfaction: 'I don't like her because she was naughty and turned off the wireless' and that she was now 'dead', but showing consternation as well. At a later date, having broken Libberbel's head, she remarked apprehensively, as if wishing to reassure herself: 'But you can't break ladies' babies.' At this time Dinah showed renewed interest in stories about stealing, hiding her head and squirming excitedly· at the climax. Once again, too, she became acutely sensitive to naughtiness, and was afraid of 'somebody naughty coming'; she was often unable to sleep and would lie awake, listening to footsteps and noises outside, while one night at bedtime when alone with her mother, she said: 'There's somebody naughty in the room, and it isn't you and it isn't me.' She often attacked her mother, then immediately kissed her better with great sympathy, saying it was an accident, and constantly followed her about as if to make sure that she had not really come to any harm.

At the height of her sadistic feelings towards her mother and her wish to take her place and have the baby herself, Dinah (3) remarked: 'Oh dear, I've got such a fat tummy! I've got two girls, two boys, and a puppy in there.' Three weeks later, however, she said she had only one tiny girl baby inside her, which was going to stay there till she was grown-up, while: 'Libberbel has a baby monkey in hers, because she's pretending to be a monkey.' Another day she announced: 'I'm so fat I've got two tummies', and when asked what they were for, replied: 'One for my baby and one for my food, of course'; while at a later date she asked: 'What's the tummy called where I keep my baby—that little bag?' About the same time the following conversation took place:

Dinah: 'I keep my baby inside my tummy because if he comes out of my tummy he might get a bit cold.'

Mother: 'When's he coming out?'

Dinah: 'When I'm a big grown-up lady.'

Mother: 'Who's his daddy?'
Dinah: 'The good pirate.'
Mother: 'And where's he?'
Dinah: 'At another house, hiding behind the bedroom door.'

Although at this time Dinah was still laying some claim to her father as a husband, and recounting such stories as: 'A mummy and a daddy and a little girl all had a bath together in a big bath and then went to bed together, the daddy in the middle', she was also talking increasingly about her husband 'the good pirate'. Her day-to-day account of his activities gave evidence of an imaginative experience which seemed to act as an escape from the urgent need for the fulfilment of her wishes in relation to her parents. She had heard about the bad pirates in *Treasure Island* who stole from ships, and invented this good one who did not steal, but instead went all the way to Africa to get oranges and bananas for her. This concept of the good pirate was evidently based on her father, who had himself at various times been absent on journeys, and would periodically return home laden with good things, and had also been at sea during the war, where he had many exciting experiences which he liked to recount. Moreover, she announced one day that the good pirate was 'a little bit Irish', which obviously related to the fact that her father came from Ireland.

It was at this point that she began to show interest in the father's sexual role, the following conversation taking place:

Dinah: 'Did we live in London when I was born?'
Mother: 'Yes.'
Dinah: 'Who put me in your tummy?'
Mother: 'Daddy.'
Dinah: 'How?'
Mother: 'How do you think?'
Dinah: 'I don't know.'

Two days later she asked again: 'How did Daddy put me in

your tummy?' and her mother explained that a little seed was put in by his 'taily'.

Dinah: 'How did he put the little seed in your tummy with his taily? Where?'

Mother: 'In the same little hole where the baby comes out.'

Dinah continued to look puzzled and changed the subject, but some days later she again asked the same question several times, and listened to the same answer with satisfaction. She also wanted to know when the baby was conceived, how her mother got into her 'mummy's tummy', and the names of her mother's parents.

When Dinah was 3.2 the family moved to a furnished cottage in the country. She at once recognized it as the house she had longed for, with white walls and apple trees in the garden, and said: 'It was winter when I used to live here with the good pirate, and the good pirate was my husband and I was the mummy, and all my babies lived there.'

Mother: 'And where was I?'

Dinah: 'You were one of my babies.'

Mother: 'And where was Daddy?'

Dinah: 'He was there too—there were two daddies.'

She added that she dressed the babies in woollies and fed them on warm milk, and that they played in their pens all day while she and Daddy and the good pirate did the cooking together. Many things in the cottage seemed to 'remind' her of this time: for instance, when no sieve could be found she said: 'Do you know why there isn't a sieve? Because I forgot to buy one when I used to live here—I only bought saucepans.' She also insisted that the good pirate was at present living in the house, up an imaginary staircase which had a green carpet, together with their baby, which had by now come out of her tummy. Earlier, she had described how he worked in a factory making Libberbel's hair; when the factory had finished making her, they rang up Dinah to tell her, and she fetched her and gave her to the good pirate, who put her in her tummy so that she could come out and be born.

A week or so later Dinah asked: 'Am I made in a factory?'

Mother: 'What do you think?'

Dinah: 'No, I'm made in your tummy.'

Mother 'Why aren't you made in a factory?

Dinah: 'Because I'm people.'

Mother: 'And what's made in a factory?'

Dinah: 'Things. Where is Libberbel made?'

Mother: 'In a factory, as a matter of fact.'

Dinah: 'No, she wasn't—she was made in my tummy. She was made in both really, in a factory *and* in my tummy. Isn't that funny?'

As quoted in Chapter III, Dinah had a theory that, as children grow up, their mothers 'grow down' into babies again. She described how Libberbel was long ago a grown-up lady, then grew down into 'a real baby', and finally into a baby doll, another story being that when Libberbel was a big lady she had two babies, then the babies grew as big as Celia (a cousin) and went away, and so Libberbel grew tiny. Furthermore, while at present the good pirate was Dinah's husband, and Libberbel her baby, when Libberbel was grown-up Dinah herself would be a tiny baby and the good pirate's daughter. Some weeks later she said: 'When I was a grown-up lady, I thought to myself I would be a little girl, but good pirate decided to stay big. When I was a little girl, I thought to myself I would be a grown-up lady all over again.' Thus in Dinah's mind the phantasy of having long ago had a husband and baby was linked with the idea of future marriage and motherhood, both acting as a reassurance against her jealousy of her mother. The significance of Libberbel was suggested by her name, which was simply a variation of Dinah's mother's name, Elisabeth. In having a baby who thus represented her mother, and who had once been a grown-up lady and herself had a baby, and would grow up and have one again in the future, it is possible that Dinah was perpetuating the image of the mother with the baby inside her, and keeping this image safe inside herself, as a good object, thus avoiding a situation in which she stole the baby from the mother and left her without one. As Libberbel grew up, she said, so she, Dinah, would grow down: that is, she would restore the mother whom she had made into a baby, giving back to her the vital material needed for growth which she was taking from her in order to grow up herself. Occasionally the father, too, was said to be going to 'grow down' into a baby as Dinah herself grew up, but generally he remained a daddy, side by side with the good pirate, which perhaps emphasizes the fact that it was the mother with whom Dinah was in rivalry, and whom she wanted and yet feared to undermine. The phantasy of having inside her a mother with a baby was further illustrated when, after defaecating, Dinah announced that she had done 'two mummy big jobs, one with a boy baby in her tummy, the other with a girl,' and that the babies would come out when they went down the plug.

Dinah was well prepared for the advent of the baby, and some weeks before the birth was discussing with her parents the fact that when her mother went to hospital, her father would be staying at home to look after her, and recalling with pleasure other occasions on which she had been left in her father's charge. She asked her mother what she had been doing before she, Dinah, was born, and her mother told her that she went to work, to do psychology. Dinah later described how when *she* was a grown-up lady and went out to do her psychology, Libberbel was quite happy because the good pirate stayed at home with her and cooked her dinner.

Concern with the problem of the new baby increased as the date of the birth approached. Dinah would often go over the facts with pleasure and interest; perhaps, too, there was the wish to convince herself that she was really pleased about it. For instance, after a visit to the clinic she exclaimed with emphatic delight: 'We've been to the clinic—do you know why? Because you've got a *baby*—growing in your tummy!' She added: 'We'd better buy some rings for our baby, because babies are very fond of playing with rings.' She asked innumerable questions about him, as: 'Is he big enough to come out yet?'; 'Has he got toe-nails? Has he got finger-nails?'; and 'Does the baby cry?' adding, when her mother replied: 'No', 'I know why he doesn't cry—because he hasn't got a mouth yet.' When she asked about the position of the baby inside the mother, and was told that it was upside down and would be born head-first, she remarked: 'What a funny thing! I wasn't upside down; I was born feet-first', another day asserting that Libberbel, too, had been born feet-first, 'because she's a very unusual baby'.

Dinah did not appear upset when she woke up one morning to find that her mother had gone off to the hospital, but announced to her father: 'I shall have a lot of work to do now, because tiny babies have no sense at all.' During the day she was busy tidying the baby's drawer and sweeping the floor, 'because there are germs in the dust', and at bedtime told her father that he need not stay and read to her because she was grown-up now. A day or two later she was teaching her dolls to drink sand and water from cups, saying: 'Their mouths are too big for bottles and buttons now.' Commenting to a friend who had come to help on what a lot of ironing there was to do for the baby, she said: 'And who's the tiny baby lady?' When the question was referred back to her, she replied: 'Mummy and me', and when asked: 'Why you as well?' answered: 'Well, the tiny baby wants two baby ladies, so they can help each other with the ironing.' That afternoon she happened to mention that it was 'rude' to stand on chairs. The friend asked: 'What's rude?' and she replied: 'To pinch and bite and stand on chairs. Little babies stand up in their high chairs. . . . Little babies think it's funny, but their mummies and daddies think it's rude. . . . I used to think it was funny when I was a little tiny baby. I *was* a little tiny baby once, you know, in Devon.' In all this, Dinah showed a need to stress to herself the fact that she was no longer a baby, and to see herself as a sensible, helpful, grown-up person in relation to the new baby, and a second mother to it. She repeated again, as if perhaps to comfort herself: 'I've got a little tiny baby girl in my tummy, and it will come out when I'm grown-up', and also once again related how 'Libberbel used to be a real baby and I was her mummy and good pirate was her daddy, and I used to go out to work to do my psychology, and to do my reading and writing in the hospital.' That afternoon when energetically scribbling, she mentioned that her mother was at that time doing 'hospital psychology', and said: 'I'm doing *my* psychology. I get very tired doing it.' Although in these ways she seemed to be taking over the mother's role, nevertheless she showed an ability to face the fact that, whereas her own baby was a phantasy, her mother's was a reality, talking constantly of her as having 'a real boy baby'. She also showed her purse to the friend, and said that she had money in it to buy food for Libberbel, but that her mother had money to buy food 'really'.

While her mother was away, Dinah tended to be demanding towards her father, in an imperious and at the same time anxious way, waking him in the night and insisting that he fetch her food, and ruthlessly attacking him in the early morning if he did not get up and get her breakfast as soon as she wanted it. She would go into his room as soon as she woke, announce 'I've come to *do* you!' and hit him hard. That behind these attitudes to him lay feelings of deprivation and resentment towards the absent mother was suggested some weeks later, after the mother's return, when Dinah remarked: 'When I was a grown-up lady and did my outdoor psychology, good pirate stayed at home and looked after Libberbel, and she got terribly hungry and cried.'

Mother: 'Why?'

Dinah: 'Because mans can't feed babies—or can they?'

Mother: 'They can give them their orange juice.'

Dinah: 'Yes, good pirate did that.'

But evidently, like Mr. Kingfinks who had no buttons on his shirt (i.e. lacked nipples), the good pirate was felt to be an inadequate substitute for the mother.

When the mother returned home after the baby's birth, Dinah's reaction at the first meeting was to turn aside from both of them. She did not seem to want to see the baby, and when her mother put him down and took her on her lap and cuddled her, asking if she had missed her, Dinah looked away from her, smiling but with tears in her eyes, and whispered: 'No'; she then climbed down, saying: 'I must go and do my work', and ran out into the garden, where she played in the sand for some time on her own. Later she came in to look at the baby, and began to repeat over and over again: 'He's a dear little baby, isn't he?' During the next few days she invented many endearments for him, calling him 'My dear little Mr. Blue-Eyes', 'My dear little sweetheart', and 'My poor little baba'. She continually stroked, kissed, and patted him 'to make him happy', and would sit and talk to him to stop him crying, show him pictures, and make him drawings. She commented on his 'dear little' hands and feet, and also on his 'taily'. One day she asked: 'What will the baby do with his taily when he's a man?'

Mother: 'What do you think?'

Dinah: 'Do wee-wee standing up in the lavatory.'

Mother: 'And what else?'

Dinah: 'Well, I will be his wife.'

Mother: 'And what will he do?'

Dinah (shyly, hiding her head): 'Well, do men help to make babies?'

Mother: 'Yes.'

Dinah: 'Do they put the babies in?'

Mother: 'Yes.'

She also asked questions about his birth, such as: 'Where's your little bag now?' adding: 'The baby makes himself a little bed inside.'

At first Dinah would be present at each feed, standing close to her mother and watching intently, with a smile of satisfaction. She was evidently fascinated with the process, and would ask many questions, as for instance how soon the baby was going to have the other 'button'. She was interested that the mother's food and drink made milk for him, and discussed whether or not she had milk in her own 'buttons', concluding: 'I don't feed Libberbel with my buttons yet because they aren't big enough.' She noticed that his mouth could not be seen while he was sucking, and was delighted to see evidence of milk on his lips when he had finished. It is likely that this attitude of genuine interest and approval sprang partly from relief that her wishes to 'carve Mummy up and take the baby out' had not taken effect, since both mother and child could be seen to be whole and functioning fully. On the other hand, her protestations of affection for the baby seemed to be over-emphasized, and it was noticeable that all endearments were followed by an uncertain, self-conscious laugh, as if they covered up other feelings.

This was borne out by the fact that, from the beginning, Dinah had an evident wish to take over the roles of both mother and baby. In the first place she insisted: 'I'm his little mummy and you're his big mummy, so he's got two mummies and he likes that', and resented being told that she was his sister. In line with her promise that she was going to be the 'tiny baby lady' and help with his care, she ran willingly to fetch nappies, cottonwool, pins, etc. She also spent a great deal of time busily cleaning the house, saying that it was 'filthly' and 'I'm a grown-up lady very busy doing all my housework.' She would rinse out the nappy pail, clean the lavatory, polish the floor, and wash the walls.

Before long, there were attempts to manage and ultimately to make herself the centre of the feeding situation. She would say: 'Put that button away and give him the other one'; 'He's had enough now'; 'He's got a windy—better not have any more.' She would kiss and fondle him during his feed to the point of disturbing him, and would also play with her mother's shoulder straps, and once suddenly kissed 'a dear little button'. On one occasion she said: 'You're a horrid mummy because you make all Mike's big jobs by giving him milk, because milk makes the big jobs. I don't think you should give him *any* more milk.' To her mother's statement: 'The big jobs aren't really horrid', she replied: 'Well, they would be to eat.' Sometimes, instead of standing by and directing the feed, she would try to divert her mother's attention by demanding food herself, by sitting on the lavatory and shouting to her mother to come and wipe her bottom, by going to the top of the house and screaming, or by running about on the cold stone floor without her shoes, which she knew worried her mother considerably. In these ways Dinah seemed to be creating a situation in which either the baby or she herself had to be neglected. The wish to displace the baby was shown directly in certain ways. For instance, for a time she would insist on running after or in front of her mother whenever she thought she was going to look at him, and on one occasion when her father offered to take Mike on to his lap she immediately climbed up there herself and refused to get off, saying that she was so tired and must have something soft to lie on. Such feelings seemed to be summed up in the heartfelt appeal: 'I wish you'd take the baby away; I don't like to have to keep on kissing him and looking at him', and in the statement: 'When I was a tiny baby, I wouldn't have liked to have another baby. I wanted to be the only one.' Her fear of the effect of these wishes to be the only one and to have the baby taken away was seen when, while her mother was one day comforting Mike, she suddenly

became frightened, saying that the kitchen was a bad room because it was dark and there might be burglars, and 'burglars
might take away babies'.

The degree to which Dinah felt deprived by the baby was
shown in many ways. One evening she complained that she did
not like him because his nappies were drying in front of the
kitchen fire, crying and saying that she was cold and could not
get warm. There was also anxiety and tears because she continually felt that she was being shut out of one room or another,
and that she could not open the doors. There were many requests
for her mother to prepare meals for her, perhaps partly as an
attempt to test her willingness to do so, as she sometimes did not
eat them in the end; she also wanted large quantities of milk, as
well as demanding the baby's gripe-water and glucose. On a day
when she had been feeling particularly deprived and miserable
with a cold, she cried for one thing after another, complaining
that she had no one to look after her during Mike's bath time, and
ended by playing a game in which she became a tiny baby who
had to be spoon-fed in a high chair, wanting to be bathed in the
baby's bath, and to have her eyes bathed with boracic. The game
of pretending to be a baby was played quite often: Dinah would
make herself a pram or cot, then 'learn' to walk and talk, eventually
'growing up'. When out, she would complain of fatigue and want
to be carried. On a day when the baby had been crying a great
deal and receiving much attention, she said when in the bath:
'I don't mind you having Mike when I'm in your tummy,
because then I can't see him and he can't see me'; while another
day she asked for milk in a bottle to suck, saying: 'I want to be
a tiny baby; how can I be a tiny baby all over again and have a
bottle to suck?' Her intense feeling that all her mother's love must
go to the baby, and that she had lost it, was shown in the fact that
whenever she was invited to sit on her mother's knee or offered
a sweet while the baby was in the room, she would be slow to

accept, saying: 'Who?' and 'What—me?' One day she came into the room while the baby was asleep elsewhere. Her mother said: 'Hullo, sweetheart!'

Dinah: 'Do you mean me or Mike?'

Mother: 'You.'

Dinah: 'I can't hear. Do you mean me or Mike?'

Mother: 'You.'

Dinah: 'I can't hear. I'm too far away.'

On another day she stood by her mother during the baby's evening feed, saying: 'I want you, Mummy, but I can't have you.'

Mother: 'But I'm here all the time.'

Dinah: 'I can't come to you. Is there a burglar coming? Don't let anyone hurt me.'

Clearly it was Dinah's sense of her own aggressive impulses towards both mother and baby that made her feel she must keep away from them, and expect not love but attack.

Underlying all Dinah's behaviour lay this deep feeling of sadness; although on the whole she kept up a bright, cheerful, and busy air, from time to time she would stand looking wistful and pathetic as her mother attended to the baby, on one occasion crying quite silently, in a mature, controlled way. She would talk nostalgically about the good pirate, whom she had not seen for a long time, but who was still in his room at the top of the green staircase, and would be coming back at Christmas, bringing many presents. One day when her mother gave her a toffee from the larder, Dinah said that the good pirate had put it there, adding sorrowfully: 'He does everything I tell him.' Whenever she talked about him she looked sad, and it seemed as if from one point of view he might have represented the loving mother of the past, who had given her all the good things she wanted, and for whom she now mourned. From a reality point of view, there was some basis for these feelings of deprivation and loss, since the mother had no help in the house, and so in spite of her efforts to continue to give Dinah the attention she had been used to before the birth of the baby, she inevitably had less time to spend with her.

As time went on, Dinah began to show less adulation of the baby, and to be able to express mixed feelings about him, saying, for example: 'I always like him and I always don't like him. I like him on Fridays and Saturdays and when the laundry comes, and'—laughing—'I *don't* like him on Fridays and Saturdays and when the laundry comes!' Hostile feelings were shown directly, too; for instance, on one occasion she remarked: 'I hate Mike because he interrupts my housework by crying!' while another time, waving a heavy brass pot about, she asked humorously: 'Shall I drop it on the baby?' and later, convinced that coughing over people always gave them colds, announced that she was going to cough on Mike's bed, which she did vigorously. Most of Dinah's hostility, however, was directed against her parents. At times she would tell them that she did not want to speak to them any more, and there were many playful attacks on them, partly in fun, but with real anger visible beneath, and with obvious intent to hurt. One day when her mother was having a bath, she smacked her on the back, saying: 'I'm bossing your big jobs.' She then became a 'naughty soldier', saying: 'I'll shoot off your legs and your eyes and your mouth', adding, in a friendly way: 'Only pretendly.' Here she seemed to be expressing a wish to be in control of and do what she liked with her mother's body, including the objects inside it—her 'big jobs'—which, in view of Dinah's current phantasy of anal birth, might be taken to represent further babies. She was mischievously disobedient and destructive, putting salt on her father's pudding and then throwing it into the rubbish bin, pouring her own milk down the sink, throwing towels in the bath and objects of all kinds on the floor, and tearing up newspapers. If she did not succeed in provoking her mother by one means, she would try another, saying:-'I'm a messer; is that naughty?' and 'I'm making a lovely mess.' One day when she threw her plate on the floor, her mother asked: 'Would good pirate do that?' at which Dinah replied: 'Not unless someone had gone away.' This suggests that once again aggressive behaviour arose directly out of the feeling of being deserted.

As in the past, side by side with open expressions of hostility, Dinah developed certain specific fears. She again became frightened of cars, and in particular of tractors, and had to be carried past them, while noises in the cottage next door worried her at night, and she would cling to her mother and beg her to stay with her, saying anxiously: 'Don't let anything horrid get at me.' That these fears really related to her own aggressive impulses was shown by her statement: 'I'm frightened when I'm naughty.' One day when she was breaking and scattering eggshells on the floor, and her mother asked: 'Do you like to be naughty sometimes?' she replied: 'Yes, very much indeed, but I'm frightened of bad Igs.' Bad Igs, who bit off children's toes if they did not wear shoes, had been invented by an uncle who was staying in the house in an attempt to cope with the problem of Dinah's insistence on running about barefoot on the stone floor when she had a cold; as already described, this was one of her ways of trying to distract her mother's attention from the baby. Dinah was evidently deeply impressed by this invention, and for some days afterwards 'bad Igs' figured largely in her phantasies. They rode on broomsticks, she said, and were rather like burglars but did not steal anything; they prevented her from looking after Mike, and from moving about; they were fond of 'big jobs' and 'wee-wees', and sometimes lived in the lavatory, from which they could not get out if one closed the lid; in general, they could be kept away by shutting doors and by good magic.

It is clear that the bad Igs represented feelings in Dinah herself which she felt to be bad. It was she who sometimes felt like a burglar with intent to steal the baby, while she would scream frantically when doors were closed, as if she had been shut out, although in fact she could open them without help. Also she herself was showing particular interest in 'big jobs' and 'wee-wees', for instance asking to see Mike's dirty nappy, and later remarking: 'If you got big job on your hand, your hand would look like a big job!' At the same time there was the feeling that 'big jobs' were 'horrid', and this, together with her defiant pride in 'making a lovely mess', and on the other hand her housework, involving a preoccupation with dirt as well as an attempt to master it, suggests phantasies of attack with faeces. There was evidence that the bad Igs stood in particular for her hostile impulses towards Mike; for instance, one day when her father was holding him she tried to stop him from doing so, and then became very anxious, saying she was afraid of a bad Ig coming. She made attempts to deny these impulses, as when she declared, but in an unconvinced way: 'Bad Igs won't really bite off the baby's toes because they're too tiny', and 'Bad Igs are only pretend, really.' Another defence against them was to fight them in the person of her mother. One day the following conversation took place:

Dinah: 'Once I was your Ig slayer.'

Mother: 'And what did you do?'

Dinah: 'I killed you. Are you still dead?'

Mother: 'No.'

Dinah (smiling in a friendly way): 'No, not really.'

Mother: 'Why did you kill me?'

Dinah: 'You were a bad Ig.'

On the other hand, the mother was also felt as a safety measure, in so far as: 'Bad Igs can't hurt me when I hold your hand. They're frightened of you and run away.' Eventually she dealt with the situation by saying that the bad Igs had got themselves little red coats with good magic in, which turned them good. Like Dinah herself, they became very busy doing the housework and washing; they would get it done during the night while the family were in bed, and would have the breakfast all ready when they came down in the morning. As Dinah had remarked two months earlier: 'I was being naughty, but now I've got good by magic.'

Dinah's need for control of her aggressive impulses was also shown in games of pretending to be a wild animal. As already quoted, she said one day: 'I'm a very naughty tiger. I'm tempted to eat people up. I'm shutting myself up in a cage'; while another time: 'I'm a Mrs. Pretend-lion. I'm a good lion. I don't eat people up, because I've put myself in a cage', her mother being told: 'You're not frightened. You're the keeper.'

At this time there was a great increase in stories about the good pirate; he was brought into almost every situation and discussed in detail. Dinah spoke of him with great conviction, as if she really felt him to be in the house, saying that if one climbed up a ladder one could see his boots under his bed in his secret room, and that he crept down in the morning to make a cup of tea before the family were up, and saw the good Igs doing the house-work. One morning she said, with an air of nervous tension: 'Good pirate is coming down *now*. He's going to fall all the way downstairs on his back.' It seems possible that this intense need to establish the reality of the good pirate resulted from the fact that from day to day Dinah was having to face the reality of her mother's baby. He seemed to stand for everything good—for an all-loving mother, and for a father who gave her everything she wanted, above all, a baby. At the same time the phantasy of the baby inside her was being experienced in vivid and concrete terms. She insisted that it was going to be born by 'the back pilly' (anus), because she could actually feel it there, describing how it 'slides', while having been woken up in the night by wetting the bed, she said she woke because she felt the baby kicking in her tummy. When playing roughly with her father, she objected to his pretence at retaliation, because the baby inside her would be 'sore all over when she comes out' if he punched or squeezed her.

Dinah described the good pirate's bedroom as being 'up there through the kitchen ceiling', where, in fact, her own bedroom was, in which for some days she had been refusing to sleep. When asked if she disliked it and would prefer another one, she agreed on the grounds that the good pirate had bought the carpet in Scotland for her when she was a grown-up lady, but not when she was a little girl. She said: 'I can't see good pirate's green stairs when I'm a little girl; they're very, very far away!' and: 'I can't quite remember when I was a grown-up lady. It was a very, very, extremely long time ago.' It seems possible that the phantasy of the good pirate, with its implications of a rival relationship with a father-figure and a rival pregnancy, had become too intensely real to be borne, and that, having brought it still further into the present by designating her own bedroom as the good pirate's secret room, she had to escape and turn for relief to the reality of being only a little girl. On the other hand, in abandoning her bedroom she was perhaps giving up her efforts to establish the phantasy in terms of here and now, and relegating it to the far-distant past to preserve it from further reality tests, thus avoiding disillusion.

In general, there was at this time a drive to distinguish between real and imaginary things. She asked: 'Are the three bears real? Are they very far away? Are they a long time ago? Is their dinner real? Is Goldilock's mummy real?' 'Is my reflection in the window really out there?' and one day when comforting Mike: 'He's crying because he thinks bad Igs are real.' At the same time Dinah turned to real things with an increased interest and delight, busily trying to construct something out of empty tins, cotton-reels, and match-boxes, and making great efforts to draw objects as they really appeared to her. Amid all the interests and satisfactions of the real world, however, she remained convinced of the reality of her imaginative life, which more directly expressed her phantasies. One day she asked: 'Are dreams real?'

Mother: 'No.'

Dinah: 'My dreams are real. They're very special secret dreams on my pillow. I put my head on the pillow and shut my eyes and think what I will dream. It's always the same dream.'

Mother: 'What is the dream?'

Dinah: 'It's a secret.'

Mother: 'And does it really happen?'

Dinah: 'Yes, but very far away.'

The fact that Dinah could make such good use of her intelligence, imagination, and creative powers, her curiosity ranging so freely and expressing itself so openly, was undoubtedly due very considerably to an environment in which instinctual pleasures were not unnecessarily thwarted, and no subject of enquiry banned or disapproved of. It was on such a basis, together with her parents' good relationship with each other and with her, and their acceptance of her feelings, that Dinah's phantasies moved forward. In general we see that good development lies not only in the ability to express phantasies in a socialized way, but above all in the development of the phantasies themselves. The living-through of phantasies implies not a mere discarding of them, as a snake shuffles off his skins, but the modification and integration of them as the centre of life.

Bibliography

I.J.P.-A. International Journal of Psycho-Analysis
B.J.M.P. British Journal of Medical Psychology
N.E.F. New Education Fellowship

BALINT, ALICE. 'Love for the Mother, and Mother-Love', *I.J.P.-A.*, Vol. XXX, 1949.

BOWLBY, JOHN. *Forty-four Juvenile Thieves: their Characters and Home Life* (Baillière, Tindall & Cox).

BRITTON, CLARE. 'Children Who Cannot Play', *The New Era in Home & School*, Vol. 26, 1945.

HEIMANN, PAULA. 'Some Notes on the Psycho-Analytic Concept of Introjected Objects', *B.J.M.P.*, Vol. XXII, 1949.

ISAACS, SUSAN. *Intellectual Growth in Young Children* (Routledge).
Social Development in Young Children (Routledge).
The Nursery Years (Routledge).
The Children We Teach (University of London Press).
Childhood and After (Routledge & Kegan Paul).
Troubles of Children and Parents (Methuen).
'The Essential Needs of Children', *The New Era in Home & School*, Vol. 27, 1946.
'The Nature and Function of Phantasy', *I.J.P.-A.*, Vol. XXIX, 1948.

—— with JOAN RIVIERE and ELLA FREEMAN SHARPE. 'Fatherless Children', *N.E.F.* Monograph No. 2.

KLEIN, MELANIE. *The Psycho-Analysis of Children* (The Hogarth Press & the Institute of Psycho-Analysis).
Contributions to Psycho-Analysis (The Hogarth Press & the Institute of Psycho-Analysis).

—— with JOAN RIVIERE. *Love, Hate and Reparation*, Psycho-Analytic Epitomes, No. 2 (The Hogarth Press & the Institute of Psycho-Analysis).

BIBLIOGRAPHY

MIDDLEMORE, MERELL, P. *The Nursing Couple* (Hamish Hamilton Medical Books).

MILNER, MARION. 'A Suicidal Symptom in a Child of Three', *I.J.P.-A.*, Vol. XXV, 1944.

PETO, ENDRE. 'Infant and Mother', *I.J.P.-A.*, Vol. XXX, 1949.

RIBBLE, MARGARET A. *The Rights of Infants* (Columbia University Press).

RICKMAN, JOHN (Editor). *On the Bringing Up of Children* (Kegan Paul, Trench & Trubner).

SEARL, M. N. 'The Psychology of Screaming', *I.J.P.-A.*, Vol. XIV, 1933.
'Play, Reality and Aggression', *I.J.P.-A.*, Vol. XIV, 1933.

USHER, RUTH. 'A Case of Stammering', *I.J.P.-A.*, Vol. XXV, 1944.

WINNICOTT, D. W. 'Children and Their Mothers', *The New Era in Home & School*, Vol. 21, 1940.
'The Observation of Infants in a Set Situation', I. J.P.-A., Vol. XXII, 1941.
'Primitive Emotional Development', *I.J.P.-A.*, Vol. XXVI, 1945.
'Getting to Know Your Baby', *The New Era in Home & School*, Vol. 26, 1945.
'What Do We Mean by a Normal Child?' *The New Era in Home & School*, Vol. 27, 1946.
'Babies Are Persons', *The New Era in Home & School*, Vol. 28, 1947.
'Pediatrics and Psychiatry', *B.J.M.P.*, Vol. XXI, 1948.
'Children's Hostels in War and Peace', *B.J.M.P.*, Vol. XXI, 1948.
The Ordinary Devoted Mother and Her Baby' (Pamphlet).

—— with CLARE BRITTON. 'The Problems of Homeless Children', *N.E.F.* Monograph No. 1, 1944.

For Product Safety Concerns and Information please contact our EU
representative GPSR@taylorandfrancis.com
Taylor & Francis Verlag GmbH, Kaufingerstraße 24, 80331 München, Germany

www.ingramcontent.com/pod-product-compliance
Lightning Source LLC
Chambersburg PA
CBHW050444280326
41932CB00013BA/2233